Praises for *HAIL MARY*

LaVell Edwards, BYU Head Football Coach 1972–2000—I thoroughly enjoyed reading *Hail Mary*, and I'm grateful Ryan took the time to write it. I can't overstate how important The Miracle Bowl victory was to the BYU football program—especially the dramatic way the victory was achieved. Ryan's recap of the game was inspiring to read and reminded me of many interesting details I had forgotten about.

Matt Braga, BYU wide receiver 1979–80—I can't think of anyone better than Ryan Tibbitts to tell the story behind the 1980 Holiday Bowl and BYU's comeback victory over SMU. As a member of the 1980 squad, Ryan always had his finger on the pulse of the players, coaches, and trainers. This isn't just a story about what happened on the field that night in San Diego but what happened off the field that led to the improbable comeback.

Clay Brown, BYU tight end/punter 1976–80—*Hail Mary* brought back many exciting memories and revealed some interesting stories of which I was unaware. It was a pleasure to read.

Jim McMahon, BYU quarterback 1977–81—I'm happy I was the first quarterback to win a bowl game for LaVell. It was certainly an exciting fourth quarter. I remember saying on that last play, "I'm gonna throw it in the end zone, and one of you better catch it. We came too far to lose this game." Now the rest is history, as is recounted so well in *Hail Mary*.

Vai Sikahema, BYU running back/return specialist 1980–81, 1984–85—I read *Hail Mary* slowly so as to savor every moment. I was amazed at the amount of detail and research that went into it. I was not aware of many of the details, but I was aware of the many successful lives born of that shared experience. I loved, loved the book!

Bruce Binkowski, Holiday Bowl Executive Director   BYU put the Holiday Bowl on the college football post-season map in the early years of the game, due to their explosive offense and last-second wins. Coach Edwards's teams appeared in the first seven games. All but one of them were down-to-the-wire nail-biters. One game determined the national championship and one became known as "The Miracle Bowl," possibly the greatest come-from-behind victory in bowl history. I loved reliving the memories of the Miracle Bowl that Ryan Tibbitts has recorded in *Hail Mary*.

Scott Collie, BYU wide receiver 1978–82—I had a chance to review *Hail Mary*, and it opened up some of my greatest memories. Holiday Bowl III will go down as the most exciting game I ever participated in and have ever seen. His account of the stories within the game and during the game week were extremely intriguing and had me often saying, "I did not know that!" I loved the book.

Scott Phillips, BYU running back 1977–80—The 1980 Holiday Bowl was the most memorable game I ever played in. It is amazing how many people still remember that game. *Hail Mary* brought back many great memories, and it was a pleasure to read.

Bart Oates, BYU center 1977, 1980–82—As you will read in *Hail Mary*, the 1980 Holiday Bowl was miraculous for me in a couple of ways. I'm pleased that Ryan Tibbitts has written this book to remind me of the many great and interesting things that happened to all of us during that memorable time. It was inspiring to me to read about it all again. There were even a few things I had not heard before.

Corey Pace, BYU Center/Long Snapper 1976, 1979–81—*Hail Mary* rekindles the great memories I have had for all of these years. December 19, 1980, was much more than just a game for me. . . . It was the night before I got married in the Los Angeles Temple. The game, the play, the extra point to win the game will always be a part of what turned out to be a rather memorable weekend. It's very easy for me to say, "There isn't a week that goes by that I don't think of the 1980 Holiday Bowl." Go Cougars!

Calvin Close, BYU offensive Lineman 1976, 1979–81—Ryan Tibbitts and I were roommates for several years at BYU, and I learned that he pays close attention to details. I'm happy he applied that skill to recap our victory in Holiday Bowl III—the biggest victory I was ever involved in. It was great to relive those memories.

Dan Plater, BYU wide receiver 1978–81—The 1980 Holiday Bowl was a life-changing experience for those who were involved in it. Memories of that game are still inspiring to many of us, and I am proud to say that I was a member of that team. I am happy that my teammate Ryan Tibbitts has recorded those wonderful memories in *Hail Mary*. It was a great read.

Lee Johnson, BYU punter and kicker 1980–84—*Hail Mary* was an excellent read. It brought back some wonderful and terrifying memories for me. Holiday Bowl III was an unbelievable comeback and victory for BYU. None of us will ever forget it.

Glen Titensor, BYU defensive lineman 1978–80—*Hail Mary* brought back many fond memories for me. I especially enjoyed reading about my former teammates and coaches and where they have gone in the many years since Holiday Bowl III.

Bill Schoepflin, BYU defensive back 1977–80—Whenever I read about or hear the story of Holiday Bowl III, or others like it, I am reminded of the power of teamwork, how coaches and teammates placed their trust in one another, applied hard work, and accomplished an amazing thing. I am thankful for the bond the Miracle Bowl created between me and my coaches and teammates, and I am thankful for the memories that one of my teammates, Ryan Tibbitts, has recorded in *Hail Mary*.

Mel Farr, BYU football manager 1977–82—I loved reading *Hail Mary*. It brought back many exciting memories of one of BYU's greatest games. I'm so proud that I was a part of that amazing comeback.

Andy Reid, BYU offensive lineman 1978–80—*Hail Mary* brought back many wonderful memories for me (and my wife) and it was a fun and easy read. It reminded me how lucky we all were to be on such a great team, with wonderful administrators and coaches. When I tell other NFL coaches that I still talk to my college coach every week, they can't believe it. Coach Edwards has been such a great mentor to me over the years.

Kyle Whittingham, Linebacker 1978–81—*Hail Mary* brought back great memories of playing football for my dad and winning Holiday Bowl III. I enjoyed reliving those stories.

Kurt Gunther, Kicker 1979–82—The Miracle Bowl was the most amazing experience in my life. I couldn't sleep for two weeks. All of those incredible feelings and goosebumps resurfaced in a real way as I read and reread Ryan Tibbitts's *Hail Mary*. Ryan was my holder on the JV squad just one year before the Miracle Bowl. He was a great athlete, teammate, and friend and certainly the right person to write this book. He had a unique ability to connect with everyone on the team. Whether you are a huge BYU football fan or not, *Hail Mary* is a must-read!

HAIL MARY

THE INSIDE STORY OF BYU'S 1980 MIRACLE BOWL COMEBACK

RYAN E. TIBBITTS
WITH A FOREWORD BY LEE BENSON

PLAIN SIGHT PUBLISHING
AN IMPRINT OF CEDAR FORT, INC.
SPRINGVILLE, UTAH

Cover photos and interior photos are courtesy of the San Diego Bowl Game Association, the Holiday Bowl, Ryan Tibbitts, and Mark A. Philbrick.

ISBN 13: 978-1-4621-1658-4

Published by Plain Sight Publishing, an imprint of Cedar Fort, Inc.,
2373 W. 700 S., Springville, UT 84663
Distributed by Cedar Fort, Inc., www.cedarfort.com

LIBRARY OF CONGRESS CATALOGING-IN-PUBLICATION DATA ON FILE

Cover design by Rebecca Greenwood and Lacey Hathaway
Cover design © 2014 by Lyle Mortimer
Edited by Heidi Doxey and Eileen Leavitt and typeset by Eileen Leavitt

Printed in the United States of America

10 9 8 7 6 5 4 3 2 1

Printed on acid-free paper

To my wonderful wife, Nan, and our children, Dillon, Darian, Bailey, Sawyer, and McCoy for their encouragement and support. I couldn't have done this without them. They even thought the game was pretty cool the first three or four times I made them watch it. Now, for some reason, they think I should move on. . . .

To Ben and Evelyn.

And to the 1980 BYU Miracle Bowl team.
Never give up.

CONTENTS

FOREWORD

Of the thousands of events I covered as a sportswriter, none is etched more clearly in my mind than one that took place on a misty night in San Diego when Jim McMahon launched a pass from midfield and, after what seemed like an eternity, Clay Brown fell on his back in the end zone with the ball in his arms and no time left on the clock. That improbable pass—from one Catholic to another, playing for the Mormon school—granted BYU its miraculous come-from-way-behind win in the 1980 Holiday Bowl.

The details are as vivid today as the night they happened:

I remember the cars U-turning. From the press box high up in the stadium's south side, I could see directly onto Friars Road, the main thoroughfare on the north, where spectators were fleeing in their cars into the night. The exodus had begun in earnest early in the fourth quarter, after SMU's running backs Craig James and Eric Dickerson (who would go on to rush for more yards in the NFL in a season than any man in history) had established unquestioned dominance. So many people were intent on beating the traffic that night that they created their own early traffic jam. But they were also obviously listening on their car radios to the play-by-play because a weird thing was happening out there on Friars Road. Cars were turning around. The stream of red taillights heading west became a stream of yellow headlights heading east, back to the stadium.

I remember a press box in stunned silence as sports writers, barred from cheering in the press box, tried to absorb what they were witnessing—a quiet broken only by the reporter from a Texas newspaper sitting immediately to my right, an NBA basketball writer who had been assigned to cover the bowl game on his way to a Spurs-Lakers game in Los Angeles. Earlier, he had shared with me what he thought of his editors for making him do what the guy on the football beat was supposed to do.

Eager to be finished, and confident of a Southern Methodist victory, he'd written his entire story by the time the fourth quarter started. All that was left to insert was the final score. By the end of the game he was kneeling on the floor, banging on his chair, moaning, "No! No! No!"

I remember interviewing McMahon in the locker room. I have never met, before or since, a more confident, self-assured, competitive athlete than Jim McMahon, who should have won BYU's first Heisman Trophy in 1980. I don't recall exactly what he said as he stood by his locker; what I do recall exactly is that as he answered my questions, and the adrenaline wore off, his hands were shaking.

I remember running into Billy Casper after the game in the stadium parking lot next to a chartered bus of BYU fans. Recognizing the man who had pulled off the greatest comeback in the history of golf's major tournaments when he overcame a seven-stroke lead with nine holes to play to beat Arnold Palmer in the 1966 US Open, I asked him how this compared to that. "Oh, this one is greater," he said. "There, I had a chance. Here, there was no chance." This is a poignant memory for me since in 2012 I had the privilege of collaborating with Billy Casper on his autobiography, *The Big Three and Me*.

I remember arriving back at the San Diego Hilton to start writing my column after the game. I opened by borrowing a line from that year's hit movie, *The Empire Strikes Back*, where Han Solo, navigating an asteroid field, says to the robot C-3PO: "Never tell me the odds."

I remember Brown catching that ball and lying flat in the end zone, Sikahema's punt return for a touchdown, Johnson's onside kick, Braga's diving end zone catch, Schoepflin's block of the last SMU punt. What I don't remember is the drama surrounding Kurt Gunther's game-winning kick or McMahon screaming at the coaches when he thought they might be throwing in the towel or the chatter between the players of the two schools during the game. Because I never knew any of that until Ryan Tibbitts told me. His insider account is like living Holiday Bowl III all over again, only this time in 3D. The game that for BYU enthusiasts everywhere and anywhere will never end—and better yet, will always end the same way—just got even more interesting.

—LEE BENSON

ACKNOWLEDGMENTS

Two things happened during the research and writing of this book that convinced me it could turn into something real.

The first was the day Lee Benson offered to write a foreword for the book. I knew then that this story might be on its way. Without Lee's continual support, advice, and encouragement, this project would still be just a file on my desktop. Lee, thank you for your help and patience. We need to continue our monthly meetings for lunch.

The second was the day my wife and I walked into the Holiday Bowl offices at Qualcomm Stadium in San Diego and met with executive director, Bruce Binkowski. When Bruce, with his always-infectious smile, opened his organization's files and stacked disks of all their photographs, news clippings, and original master tapes of game footage and highlight films on the table and then said, "Here, take it all. Use it with your book however you like. We like this project," I knew the project was a go. Bruce, I hope this final product makes you proud. Thanks for all of your help and patience. Thanks to Tom Holmoe for telling me I should contact Bruce in the first place.

Next, thanks to the members of the Miracle Bowl team—many of whom have made comments on this work and the legacy of that bowl game, especially Jim, Clay, Matt, and Vai—who early on gave me their comments and support. Even if this book had not been published, it was still worth it to reconnect with all of you and hear your stories. Thanks to the team for your courage and effort on December 19, 1980, and for remaining my friends for these many years since. Thanks to Coach LaVell Edwards for being a father figure, friend, and mentor to us all.

Thanks to the people who reviewed the manuscript and made encouraging and helpful comments along the way. These people include my family; Amy Williams, who provided early edits and comments; Doug

Anderson; Dave Loyens—who also generously supported the companion video project; Dave Ostler; Henry Glasheen; Steve Hill; Carla Coonradt; Mitch Bailey; Mike Carlston; Jim Parkinson; and some others I am surely forgetting. Thanks to Shirley Johnson for her support, wealth of information, and lists of telephone numbers and email addresses for the 1980 team.

Finally, thanks to the Cedar Fort team, including my patient and kind editor, Lynnae Allred. Thank you for your great work and for being a champion of this project from your opening pitch to the Cedar Fort team to the final product. Thanks to the rest of the team: Rebecca and Lacey for the great cover, Eileen, Heidi, Lyle, and Spencer. And thanks to your partner, Kevin Doman, of HomeSports, for the introductions and unbridled enthusiasm from our first meeting to the present.

INTRODUCTION

This story began to take shape in the BYU locker room about thirty minutes after the unbelievable conclusion of the 1980 Holiday Bowl in what was then known as San Diego Stadium in California. The Miracle Bowl, as it came to be known, had just concluded with a seemingly routine extra point kick, following a spectacular forty-one yard Hail Mary pass from BYU's all-American quarterback Jim McMahon to his all-American tight end, Clay Brown.

The scene of Brown coming down with McMahon's Hail Mary heave in the decorated Holiday Bowl end zone is etched in the memory of nearly every BYU fan who was alive at the time—and even some who were born later. For well over three and a half quarters, SMU had more or less pummeled BYU. Brown's no time-on-the-clock touchdown ended one of the most dramatic, improbable comebacks in college football history as BYU overcame a 45-to-25 deficit in the last four minutes of the game.

Everyone, from the coaches on down, was in near shock at what had just happened. In just a few minutes on the game clock, the team, and BYU fans around the world, had gone from agony to ecstasy. BYU nation had been given a gift that would keep them talking for decades. Many fans, those who had attended the game and those watching at home, opened themselves up to scorn for leaving the game or turning off the television before the final four-minute rally. A common question heard around Provo and among BYU fans everywhere over the following days and weeks was, "Did you stay for (or watch) the comeback?"

As a member of that 1980 BYU team, I can still remember the stunned atmosphere in the locker room as the team tried to calm down and get dressed for the flight home. Some of the players and staff were in tears, some were in a daze of disbelief, and some were ecstatic with the energy generated by the unbelievable comeback and miraculous ending.

There is no way to accurately put into words the human electricity and range of emotions in the locker room that night. McMahon described the locker room as "delirious," which probably nails it as well as anything.

The Hail Mary play is credited for forty-one yards, but after you count McMahon's drop back and add six or seven yards of end zone, the pass covered sixty yards. McMahon lofted the pass from the BYU forty-seven yard line and threw it about as high and far as he could throw it. Brown came to rest deep in the end zone, which helps explain why people who observed it remember the pass being suspended in the air for what seemed like an eternity.

The "Hail Mary" moniker likely originated, at least in a football context, with the famed Four Horsemen of the University of Notre Dame, who played in the 1930s and pulled out their fair share of unlikely comeback victories. It came to denote any kind of a successful last-second desperation play, punctuated with some sort of implied supplication to heaven. The name gained legs and came to signify a long, last-hope pass attempt after NFL Hall of Famer Roger Staubach won a playoff game for the Dallas Cowboys in 1975 against the Minnesota Vikings by heaving a last-second bomb that wide receiver Drew Pearson caught near the goal line and then coasted into the end zone for the winning touchdown. Staubach, a Catholic, explained the stunning play by saying, "I closed my eyes and said a Hail Mary."

It is unlikely that the BYU faithful were literally thinking "Hail Mary" as the play unfolded, but there is little doubt that prayers of many varieties were being uttered on the sidelines and by fans of both teams. In the end, the BYU fans could not believe what they had just witnessed.

The McMahon-to-Brown Hail Mary pass garnered headlines around the country the next day. Even though the game had not been carried by a major television network (it had been broadcast by The Mizlou Network), word of the miraculous BYU comeback spread through the sports world overnight. The headline from the *Daily Californian* read: "'Hail Mary' pass results in 'Mormon Miracle' as BYU slips past Mustangs."[1] The *Wisconsin State Journal* proclaimed, "BYU prayer answered with 'Hail Mary' pass."[2] The *Atlanta Journal* declared, "'Hail Mary' pass clinches BYU's first bowl victory."[3] Another headline read, "Saints get a 'miracle' to win 46–45."[4] The *Arizona Republic* declared, "BYU victory hailed as holiday miracle."[5] Sportswriter Lee Benson, of the *Deseret News*, called the game "The Houdini Bowl."[6] The *San Diego Tribune* asked, "Do you believe in miracles? BYU does."[7] The 1980 Holiday Bowl McMahon-to-Brown pass is now cited as one of only a few examples under the Wikipedia listing for "Hail Mary Pass."

The writer for the *Daily Californian* gushed, "Remember Franco Harris's 'Immaculate Reception' of several years ago? Well, Friday's game-winner at least matched it."[8] That is quite a compliment considering the accolades the "Immaculate Reception" game continues to garner. In the October 22, 2012, issue of *Sports Illustrated*, an article entitled "Football's Greatest From 1 to 10." The article lists ten categories such as Best Quarterback, Best Receiver, Best Coach, and so on. Within each category the ten best selections are ranked. The Immaculate Reception is highlighted as the number one Best Play in NFL history.[9] Although the Holiday Bowl Hail Mary generated some of the same type of hysteria at the time, given the implications the Immaculate Reception had for the NFL playoffs that year and the ongoing debate and analysis that memorable play still generates, it is difficult to say that the Hail Mary in Holiday Bowl III has reached that same stature as a play—except possibly for BYU fans. In fact a complete episode of "A Football Life" from 2012 on the NFL Network was dedicated to the December 1972 "Immaculate Reception." It should also be noted that the play is called the "Immaculate Deception" by the Raiders and their fans—and that debate still rages.

The efforts of McMahon and Brown on that final Hail Mary pass are well chronicled. There is just no getting around the improbability of that play—and the comeback that led up to it. McMahon's ability to rally and lead his team to victory propelled him into the college football limelight and set him up for another record-setting (although injury marred) senior season at BYU. It also helped land him near the top of the 1982 Heisman race and NFL draft. Not long after the game, BYU head Coach LaVell Edwards predicted that McMahon would lead an NFL team to the Super Bowl someday. It only took McMahon four seasons in the NFL to fulfill LaVell's prediction.

Brown was both an outstanding tight end and punter for BYU. He led the nation in punting in 1979 with a 45.3-yard average, and he was also the all–Western Athletic Conference first team tight end. He earned all-American honors in his senior season, but his performance in the 1980 Holiday Bowl and "the catch" moved him up on draft boards with NFL teams, putting him in play to be drafted in the second round by the Denver Broncos in 1981. Even before the miracle catch, Brown had distinguished himself in the Holiday Bowl. In the closing minutes of the game, Brown made a reception and long run down the sideline to the SMU fifteen yard line, causing the play-by-play announcer Ray Scott to declare, "Although in a losing effort, Clay Brown has put on quite a show." Color commentator Grady Alderman then added, "He really is something special as a tight end."

Following Brown's final touchdown, BYU's sophomore placekicker, Kurt Gunther, trotted onto the field and nailed the extra point that provided the margin of victory for BYU: one point, 46 to 45. It was the first time in the game that BYU was in the lead, and it only happened after time had run out on the game clock. Following Gunther's game-winning kick, pandemonium erupted as BYU fans, at least those who were still at the game, stormed the field. Given the slaughter the BYU fans suffered through for the first three-plus quarters of the game, many of them had started leaving the stadium in the third quarter. Some have estimated that only half of the original 52,000 fans remained by the time the game ended. That may be true, but as BYU lined up for the final Hail Mary play, we all heard a loud chant in the stadium, "BYU . . . BYU . . . BYU."

After the wild, post-game celebration on the field waned a bit, the BYU team headed for the locker room where the celebration continued in a truncated fashion because the team needed to hurry to the San Diego airport to catch the flight back to Utah.

HAIL MARY PASS

A Hail Mary pass or Hail Mary route is a very long forward pass in American football, made in desperation with only a small chance of success, especially at or near the end of a half.[1]

In the 1980 Holiday Bowl, BYU was down 45–25 with four minutes left in the game. Quarterback Jim McMahon spearheaded a last-gasp come-from-behind victory, capping the comeback with a successful Hail Mary pass to tight end Clay Brown as time expired. This touchdown tied the game. Kurt Gunther's extra point kick gave BYU its first-ever bowl win, defeating SMU 46–45.

Among BYU fans this game is still known as the Miracle Bowl.

1. https://en.wikipedia.org/wiki/Hail_Mary_pass

THE SET-UP

The BYU equipment manager at the time of Holiday Bowl III was Floyd Johnson, a great old gentleman, who was the most passionate missionary for BYU and the LDS church that any of the BYU players had ever known. BYU is a private university founded, supported, and guided by the Church of Jesus Christ of Latter-day Saints, and as part of the university mission, sports teams often sponsor "firesides." These are evening meetings where players speak to small gatherings of church members and interested people in the community. Floyd coordinated the fireside program for the football team and made assignments to various team members to speak to the people who attended these firesides. The theme of these meetings was usually to have several members of the team and coaching staff share faith-promoting experiences about their conversion to or membership in the church, or to share experiences about how being a football player, getting an education, or providing service to other people contributed to their ability to be a good Christian.

Partly because of his assignment to arrange these meetings, Floyd was acutely aware of and constantly in search of opportunities to connect BYU football with the larger mission of the university. While the post-game celebration was reaching a crescendo in the locker room, Floyd blurted out, "If that doesn't give you a testimony, nothing will!" I knew Floyd well enough to know that he was not really saying that the victory should give someone a testimony of the LDS church or the gospel, he was simply caught up in the rapture of the moment and was trying as best he could to give voice to the unbelievable, unexplainable ending he had just witnessed.

Floyd worked his way around the locker room hugging anyone in sight. When he got to me, I said, "I'm not sure what it proves about religion, Floyd; remember, McMahon and Brown are Catholics, Bill Schoepflin (who blocked the punt that gave BYU the ball back with thirteen seconds to play) and Matt Braga (who caught an earlier touchdown to fuel the comeback) are both Catholics too." I continued, "In the game between the Mormons and the Methodists, the Catholics won!" Floyd smiled politely, mumbled something under his breath, and moved on through the jubilant locker room.

My comment about the Mormons, Methodists, and Catholics seemed catchy to me, so I filed it away in my memory and used it many times over the next weeks and months (and even years), when anyone tried to explain the BYU bowl victory as some kind of divine intervention. I could usually get some good laughs at firesides or other speaking engagements with that story.

A year later I was in my first year of law school at BYU and was still occasionally asked to speak at firesides or other functions about the game and my experiences as a member of that BYU football team. At that time it was an annual tradition at the law school to invite the head football and basketball coaches to speak at "brown bag" luncheons during their respective seasons. Law students and faculty would fill up the moot court room and listen to the coaches talk about their respective sports as a break from briefing cases and worrying about all-or-nothing final exams.

Head football Coach LaVell Edwards was always a popular draw for the luncheon series. He was and is a witty and compelling speaker and has always enjoyed the back and forth with the law students in a question-and-answer session—usually with his tongue firmly planted in his cheek. For example, at the time of Holiday Bowl III, Coach Edwards was regularly taken to task in the press and by fans because he avoided trickery on the field, such as fake punts, reverses, and other so-called "trick" plays. When he opened the brown bag session up to questions, one law student, no doubt trying to sound impressive to the crowd, queried, "Coach, do you have an aversion to deception or why don't you ever run trick plays?" Without much hesitation, and feigning deep contemplation, Coach Edwards replied, "I guess you could say I have an aversion to deception—which is why I never considered becoming a lawyer." Of course, most everyone laughed hysterically, and that exchange extinguished any further questions designed to put coach on the spot.

Because I had been on his team for a couple of years, the law school organizers of the luncheon asked me to introduce Coach Edwards to the crowd. I proudly complied with the request. In the process of the introduction, I told my, by then, well-worn story that in the battle between the Mormons and Methodists, the Catholics had won. I was flattered by the laughter I received from the crowd of law students and faculty. As a lowly first year law student, I was really trying to impress them.

When Coach Edwards took the microphone, he quickly clarified, "Wait a minute, Ryan. Remember, the Catholics only tied the game. It took a returned LDS missionary, Kurt Gunther, to actually win the game for us!" The moot court room exploded with laughter. In one stroke, Coach Edwards had trumped my Mormons, Methodists, and Catholics joke.

I knew full well, of course, that there were many LDS players on both sides of the ball for BYU whose efforts were crucial to our victory that night in San Diego. Running back Scott Phillips scored fourteen points with two touchdowns and a two-point conversion. Phillips also caught ten passes, which set a Holiday Bowl record, and he was really a workhorse for the team out of the backfield throughout the game. In one important play that is often overlooked, on the second BYU play from scrimmage in the game, Jim McMahon attempted a pass down the field. SMU nose tackle Michael Carter blocked the pass, which flipped up in the air. SMU linebacker Byron Hunt was right under the ball and would have intercepted it, but Phillips had the presence of mind to get a hand on the ball and knock it away just as it settled into Hunt's hands. As bad as the first half was for BYU, an interception on the second play of the game, deep in BYU territory, would have likely led to an even worse disaster.

Vai Sikahema, a freshman running back and kick-return specialist, scored on an 83-yard punt return just before the half to breathe some life into the moribund Cougars. Corey Pace was the long snapper for the game-winning extra point.

Many players on the starting offensive line were LDS, including center Bart Oates and guards Lloyd Eldredge and Calvin Close—all three of whom had served two-year proselyting missions for the Church of Jesus Christ of Latter-day Saints. Tackles Nick Eyre and Ray Linford were LDS, as was middle linebacker Kyle Whittingham, who had a game high ten unassisted tackles. Glen Redd, Glen Titensor, and Mark Brady, who were also standouts on defense, were LDS, as were many others. Freshman kicker Lee Johnson pulled off a clutch on-side kick, which was critical in the comeback too. Yet, I had chosen not to let those facts get in the way of a good joke.

It is an interesting contrast between the BYU teams from that era and today that on the starting offensive and defensive units for BYU in 1980 there were only four returned LDS missionaries: Eldredge, Close, and Oates on the offensive line and Brad Anae on the defensive line. None of the so-called skilled position starters (quarterbacks, receivers, backs, defensive backs) on the 1980 team were returned missionaries. There were several returned missionaries on the special teams, including Corey Pace and Kurt Gunther.

For many years, it was considered a weakness for BYU to allow its players to serve two-year missions, as it was thought they would lose their edge, be too out of shape to play, or otherwise lose the desire to play the physical game of football. Those things are all factors for some players, but for others the two years away from the sport allows them to grow and develop more, possibly improving their game. As more and more BYU players began to serve missions and then come back and succeed on the football field, BYU was often accused of using the mission program to enhance the football program. Ultimately, because a mission can be a plus and a minus as far as football is concerned, the theory that BYU supported the LDS mission program only as a way to gain a competitive advantage in football was proved to be a fallacy. These days many universities around the country have returned missionaries on their rosters in various sports. That eighteen-month- to two-year-mission hiatus is now just considered a fact of life when recruiting many LDS athletes.

In 2000 BYU held a twenty-year reunion for the 1980 Miracle Bowl squad. The university hosted the team for a nice dinner and invited team members to accept applause on the stage of the BYU Homecoming Spectacular in the Marriott Center. Later we were escorted onto the field at halftime of the homecoming game to watch highlights of the 1980 Holiday Bowl on the big screen and receive another ovation. It was a wonderful experience for us—even if it was shocking to see how old, bald, and paunchy many of us had become. During the various festivities, I had the chance to talk to my old teammates and catch up on everyone's lives since our days wearing the royal blue uniforms.

When I talked to Kurt Gunther, I told him about my experience at the law school luncheon years before with Coach Edwards. He laughed and said, "I know. Every time I see Coach he tells me that story with a gleam in his eye." Kurt and I were on the BYU JV football team during the 1979 season, and I had been his holder for PATs and field goals, so we had bonded over those experiences before Kurt became the varsity place-kicker. We had a good laugh at those memories.

Every year during the spring football practice schedule, the football coaches and athletic department hold a barbeque and reception for former players and their families. They invite us to a closed scrimmage and encourage us to get back in touch with our BYU football roots. In 2011 I realized I had not attended the spring festivities for several years. I happened to have a free date on my schedule, so I took my family to the barbeque and scrimmage. One of the former players I met on the sidelines during the scrimmage was Kurt Gunther. Kurt and I again reminisced and had some laughs about our football days at BYU.

As often happens, the talk turned to the 1980 Holiday Bowl. I reminded him of my ill-fated Mormons, Methodists, and Catholics joke, and we laughed again at the story of how Coach Edwards had one-upped me at the law school luncheon. Kurt then told me a few things about his game-winning kick in 1980 that I had not heard before. Among other things (as I will explain later) he was focused on keeping his eye on the ball. He knew that if he took his eyes off the ball—one of the most common mistakes in many sports, including golf, tennis, baseball, soccer, and American football—he would likely not succeed in the attempt. The pressure on him had been intense. I was surprised to learn that in addition to the pressure of the moment and just closing out the win in the miraculous comeback, several other problems presented themselves as Kurt took the field and attempted that game-winning kick.

The television announcer of the 1980 Holiday Bowl game for the Mizlou Network, famed sportscaster Ray Scott, probably had no idea how true his observation was shortly after the final McMahon-to-Brown touchdown. He said: "The pressure is now all on this BYU special team." If he'd only known what was really going on in Gunther's head at the time, Scott may have dwelt on that point even longer. True, there was pressure all along the BYU line— for the long-snapper, Corey Pace, and the holder, Bill Schoepflin. But the full weight of that tension fell squarely on the shoulders of 5'10" 170 pound Kurt Gunther as he ran on the field in his size-seven soccer shoes.

Much has been written about the heroics of McMahon and Brown in tying the game with no time on the clock, about Sikahema's punt return for a touchdown, about Braga's diving touchdown reception, and about Schoepflin blocking the punt that gave BYU the ball in scoring position with thirteen seconds to play. Each of those plays was spectacular in its own right. Not as much has been written or said about the mini-drama that was playing out in Gunther's head as he took to the field to kick an extra point that would ensure that everything that preceded it would not be obscured by a tie.

As he joined the final huddle that night, with the score tied 45 to 45, with no time on the clock, after one of the most dramatic comebacks in college football history—certainly the most dramatic comeback in BYU football history—in a televised post-season bowl game, Kurt was not thinking of glory or victory. He told me he was thinking about the place-kicker for BYU the year before and the ending of the prior year's Holiday Bowl. I was stunned at what he told me. I simply could not believe it and said something along the lines of, "You're kidding me, right? *That* is what you were thinking about? Are you *serious*?" He assured me he was. After hearing him describe the details of what was going on in his head, I'm a little surprised he was willing to take the field at all.

THE HOLIDAY
BOWL

To fully appreciate what was weighing on Kurt Gunther's shoulders and on the shoulders of the entire BYU football program that December night in 1980, it helps to understand the early history of the Holiday Bowl and BYU's somewhat tortured part in it.

The work to bring an NCAA-sanctioned game to San Diego began in 1977, shortly after the Fiesta Bowl cut its ties with the Western Athletic Conference. Arizona State and the University of Arizona had both recently left the WAC to join the PAC-Eight, leaving the Phoenix-based Fiesta Bowl without close geographic ties to the conference. Seeing a void to be filled, the Greater San Diego Sports Association, with new WAC member San Diego State in its backyard, pursued a feasibility study and on December 15, 1977, the decision was made to go ahead full speed to bring a bowl game to the San Diego area.

A presentation was made to the NCAA in January 1978 in Atlanta, and by April the game was formally approved. It was christened the "Holiday Bowl" because people think of the San Diego area as a place for taking holidays and vacations and because the game was to be played during the Christmas season. Momentum for bringing a bowl game to San Diego was fostered by an article written a year earlier by Jack Murphy, of the *San Diego Union*, where he observed, "There will be 15,000 empty hotel rooms here in December. A bowl game would do great things for our industry." The people of San Diego did not forget Murphy's contributions, which also included lobbying to bring the Chargers, then of the old

American Football League, from Los Angeles to San Diego. When the longtime sports editor died on September 24, 1980, a movement began to change the name of San Diego Stadium to Jack Murphy Stadium.

Following the holiday theme, the poinsettia was chosen as the logo for the new bowl. The Holiday Bowl became the automatic bowl bid for the WAC champion—to replace the Fiesta Bowl. Originally the WAC champion played an at-large team and later the bowl became affiliated with the Big Ten conference.[1]

Stan Bates, commissioner of the Western Athletic Conference at the time, expressed great pleasure in welcoming the Holiday Bowl to the postseason NCAA schedule: "Speaking for the entire conference, we are extremely happy to have the continued opportunity to exhibit to the nation the caliber of WAC football via the Holiday Bowl. The people of San Diego city, [San Diego] county, and at San Diego State University, our newest member, are to be congratulated on their hard work in obtaining NCAA certification."[2]

Bruce Binkowski, the Holiday Bowl's current executive director, who has been with the Holiday Bowl since the beginning, remembered that the idea behind getting a bowl game to San Diego was to showcase the San Diego State University Aztecs in much the same way the Fiesta Bowl had been a showcase for Arizona and Arizona State. "Then," he laughed, "BYU came to the first seven games."[3]

The Holiday Bowl was destined to become an integral part of BYU football lore. In 1984, thanks to a win in Jack Murphy Stadium over Michigan, the bowl yielded a national championship to the Cougars. For years, San Diego was considered BYU's vacation home every December. Through 2012 the Cougars had played in eleven Holiday Bowls, by far the most appearances of any school. Texas came in second with five appearances. A book commemorating the first twenty-five years of the Holiday Bowl, published by the San Diego Bowl Game Association, is entitled *Miracles and Memories 25 Years of Holiday Bowl Magic*. In that book, the 1980 bowl is appropriately called "a game for the ages." Eight former Cougar players are members of the Holiday Bowl Hall of Fame—four of them from the 1980 team: Jim McMahon, Clay Brown, Bart Oates, and Kyle Whittingham. The other players are Ty Detmer, Steve Young, Robbie Bosco, and Leon White. Coach Edwards is also in the Holiday Bowl Hall of Fame, as is Craig James from the 1980 SMU team.

Holiday Bowl I—December 22, 1978
Brigham Young University vs. Navy

But the legacy was slow to develop. BYU's first appearance in the inaugural Holiday Bowl of 1978 was against the United States Naval Academy—if a city full of sailors couldn't get the hometown Aztecs into the game, they went with the next best thing—and while the contest started favorably for the Cougars, this time the comeback was orchestrated by the team on the other side of the ball. BYU dominated the first half, punctuated by a goal-line stand that denied Navy a touchdown as time expired. Then the Cougars added a touchdown in the third quarter to go up 16–3. That's when a Navy team that had been sound asleep woke up and ran off twenty straight points. The backbreaker was a 65-yard pass-and-run touchdown from Midshipmen receiver Phil McConkey, who would go on to win a Super Bowl ring with the New York Giants. The BYU offense, with quarterbacks Marc Wilson and Jim McMahon alternating in the game, as they had all season, gained a grand total of 16 offensive yards in the final twelve minutes after McConkey's score.

At that point in its history, BYU had played in just two bowl games—the 1974 Fiesta Bowl and 1976 Tangerine Bowl, both losses. After Navy's comeback, BYU was still 0-for-forever in bowl games. The season ended with Coach Edwards vowing he would never again alternate quarterbacks, a promise he kept in 1979 when he redshirted McMahon and gave the reins to Wilson—with spectacular results.

Holiday Bowl II—December 21, 1979
Brigham Young University vs. University of Indiana

The 1979 BYU football season was, up to that point, the greatest season that a BYU football team had ever had. BYU ran the table in the regular season and outscored opponents 447 to 125. Quarterback Marc Wilson, who would earn first-team all-American honors and become a first-round NFL draft pick, began the season by engineering a dramatic come-from-behind victory over fourteenth-ranked Texas A&M in College Station, Texas. BYU went on to win the Western Athletic Conference championship without really being tested, and the 12-0 Cougars received an invitation to play the University of Indiana in Holiday Bowl

II in San Diego. Along the way, BYU led the nation in total offense, passing offense, and scoring offense with more than forty points a game. In the final game of the regular season, which was nationally televised as an ABC Game of the Week, BYU embarrassed San Diego State 63 to 14 and ended the regular season ranked number nine in the nation. In that game BYU scored its 63 points in 66 plays.

For Cougar fans, that nationally televised blowout victory made it feel like BYU had finally arrived for good on the national college football scene. The stage was set for a glorious, year-ending trip to the Holiday Bowl to avenge the previous year's Holiday Bowl loss to Navy, finish off the year undefeated, and ensure a top-ten and possible top-five ranking in the nation.

There was every reason to believe that BYU would finally win a post-season bowl game after their three prior unsuccessful attempts. They were up against an Indiana team that had concluded the regular season with a 7-4 record and just a fourth place finish in the Big Ten.

But the underdog Hoosiers played well and with a chip on their shoulders. The game was a see-saw battle with the teams trading scores throughout. The lead changed hands seven times. Wilson passed for 380 yards and two touchdowns, but he was intercepted twice. BYU generated 520 yards of total offense, and the teams combined for 874 total yards. At halftime the score was 21–17 for the Hoosiers. BYU's offense was not really stopped by the Hoosiers, but interceptions, fumbles and other miscues did plenty of damage. Indiana scored ten points as a result of BYU turnovers.

With twelve minutes to play, BYU took the lead, 37–31, on a twenty-eight-yard Brent Johnson field goal. Despite all the mistakes, it appeared BYU might escape with a victory and complete a perfect season. Johnson had been perfect for BYU during the game, making three field goals—including one from forty-six yards out—and converting all of the extra point attempts. He had scored 13 out of the 37 points for the Cougars. In his senior season, Johnson had been an outstanding performer for BYU, the leading scorer on this prolific scoring team. Johnson earned all–Intermountain West honors as a kicker for the season. When people thought of Johnson as the BYU kicker, "dependable" was the word that came to mind.

Late in the fourth quarter, BYU was in a punting situation. Clay Brown punted the ball for the Cougars, and it looked for a moment like

Indiana would let the ball bounce until it was downed by BYU. Then, unexpectedly, the football took an erratic hop and hit a Hoosier player in the back, which made it a live ball. Indiana's star defensive back, Tim Wilbur, who was already running at near full-speed, grabbed the ball off of the ricochet and sprinted 62 yards for an Indiana touchdown and, with the extra point, a 38–37 Hoosiers lead. With 2:06 left to play, BYU got the ball back, and Wilson moved the offense nearly seventy yards down the field. With eleven seconds to play, Brent Johnson ran out for what appeared to be an easy, chip shot field goal from twenty-seven yards out to win the game. As much as or more than anyone, Johnson had contributed to make this moment possible with the three field goals and four extra points he had already made. If he had not been so dead-on during the game, BYU would not have been in a position to win.

On the other hand, if costly mistakes had not been made by other BYU players during the game, Johnson would not have needed to save the game at the end. But that is the lonely spot kickers often find themselves in. He could've made this kick with his eyes closed—or so the saying goes. In this case, the saying was terribly wrong. Johnson miss-hit the ball and missed the field goal. Indiana ran the clock out for the victory.

In one sense, Johnson was a victim of his team's success in 1979. Other than the one-point victory over Texas A&M to begin the season, which BYU won on a daring two-point conversion pass from Marc Wilson to tight end Mike Lacey, the next closest game BYU had that year was a 31 to 17 victory over Long Beach State. In other words Johnson, who in his junior season in 1978 had won two games for BYU—over New Mexico and Oregon—with last-minute successful field goals, was never called upon in that 1979 season to win a game or to make any pressure-filled kicks at all.

To his credit Johnson accepted full responsibility for the miss. He explained that the snap and the hold were good, but he just missed the kick. He said he punched it and did not follow through. And, as is the lot for kickers everywhere, if you miss what would have been the game-winning kick, no one remembers or talks about the many points you scored earlier in the game, and no one remembers the interceptions and fumbles that made the score so close in the first place.

Coach Edwards bravely tried to deflect the criticism from Johnson by saying that the loss could not be blamed on the kicker and pointed to other costly mistakes made throughout the game.

By all standards, the 1979 BYU team had an unbelievable year. Quarterback Marc Wilson was a consensus all-American, finished third in the Heisman trophy voting, and was drafted in the first round by the Oakland Raiders. Many other Cougars were named to the all-WAC Team and various all-American teams. The team finished at the top of the statistics nationally in many offensive categories—including all the major ones. Nevertheless, the '79 team is almost forgotten in BYU lore because of its disappointing loss in the bowl game. Even though the team went 11-1 and finished ranked thirteenth in the nation, the season is not usually mentioned as one of the more successful years for BYU football. One can't help but wonder if BYU had won the bowl game where that team would stack up in the list of great BYU teams. The 1979 Cougars would have been undefeated at 12-0, victorious in a bowl game, and ranked in the top ten in the nation. That season would have been considered one of the top seasons ever for BYU football.

The night before that 1979 bowl game, tight end Clay Brown's wife dreamed that he caught the game-winning touchdown pass. Although Brown caught nine passes in the game from Wilson, there was no game-winning catch for Brown and no victory for the Cougars. The dream would have to wait.

Holiday Bowl III—December 19, 1980
Brigham Young University vs. Southern Methodist University

If the 1980 Holiday Bowl between Brigham Young University and Southern Methodist University is not the most important football game in BYU history, it is certainly in the top two or three.

You could argue that BYU's 1984 Holiday Bowl victory over the Michigan Wolverines to give BYU the national championship should be at the top of the list. It was an extremely exciting—BYU fans would say nerve-wracking—game, with quarterback Robbie Bosco playing on an injured knee. It wasn't until the last few seconds that the victory was sealed with a Bosco to Kelly Smith pass. But it rarely makes any football expert's list of bowl classics.

The 1997 Cotton Bowl Classic (1996 season), which was BYU's first New Year's Day bowl game, ended with a 19-15 last-minute victory over Kansas State, solidifying the Cougars with a number 5 final ranking for the season. That game certainly deserves to be in the discussion too—although it has not acquired the same kind of legacy as either the '80 or '84 Holiday Bowls.

But the 1980 Miracle Bowl was BYU's first post-season bowl victory and confirmed the Cougars as a team that could defeat teams from the powerful conferences. BYU's victories in Holiday Bowl III over SMU, Holiday Bowl IV over Washington State (Another McMahon nail biter, where BYU won 38 to 36) and the Steve Young-engineered come-from-behind victory over Missouri in the 1983 Holiday Bowl set the table for BYU's national championship run in 1984. Without those three prior bowl victories over teams from powerful conferences, the '84 Cougars likely would not have been named national champions, despite their perfect season. The undefeated 1984 effort was certainly worthy of the national championship on its own, but the success of the teams before 1984 gave the program credibility that helped close the deal when it came time for championship voting.

SMU brought a storied football program to the 1980 Holiday Bowl, with deep and pedigreed roots, dating back to 1915. The Mustangs won conference championships in the 1920s and attended their first bowl game in 1924: the New Year's Day Dixie Bowl in Dallas, Texas. The Dallas school went on to win a national championship in 1935, followed by more conference championships in the 1940s. And in 1948 running back Doak Walker was awarded a Heisman trophy. That same year the Mustangs began playing their games in the Cotton Bowl Stadium, which was nicknamed "The House that Doak Built." When Walker moved on to the NFL, he was replaced by yet another celebrated all-American running back, Kyle Rote. The Walker/Rote era was followed in the 1950s and 1960s with teams that featured players who would gain fame in the NFL, among them Don Meredith, Forrest Gregg, Raymond Berry, Jerry LeVias, and Chuck Hixson. LeVias, who was the first African-American to receive a scholarship in the Southwest Conference, led SMU to an Astro-Bluebonnet Bowl Victory over Oklahoma in 1968 and earned all-American and academic all-American honors. The 1970s were a relatively quiet period for SMU football until Ron Meyer was hired in 1976 and began to build the juggernaut that would soon be known as The Pony Express.

While BYU fans and other subjective observers routinely use the lofty "Miracle Bowl" moniker to refer to the 1980 Holiday Bowl, I suspect that fans of Southern Methodist University refer to the game by some other name—if they refer to it at all. However, the game does appear on the list of the ninety greatest moments in SMU football, according to the official website of Mustang athletics, coming in at number seventy-eight. The final catch is explained in this understated manner, the "pass found its way into the arms of tight end Clay Brown for a touchdown."[4] And most of the postmortem deals with the fact that the Mustangs used the loss in the 1980 bowl as motivation the following season, where they finished 10-1, won the Southwest Conference, and ended up ranked number five in the country.

There is no mention of miracles or Hail Mary passes. In fact, the description of the last pass appears to be very carefully worded so as to not run afoul of SMU defensive back Wes Hopkins's curious claim that he caught the ball on the final pass, not Brown. Still, the game is referred to as a "stunning loss" for the Mustangs. The entry concludes as follows: "An all-time classic, the 1980 SMU-BYU game was rated the 43rd Greatest Game in College Football History by The College Football News and has been reshown a number of times on ESPN Classic. For these reasons, the 1980 Holiday Bowl appearance takes its place on our list of the 90 Greatest Moments in SMU Football History."[5]

BYU defensive back Tom Holmoe played with SMU's Michael Carter on the 49ers in the mid-1980s. Holmoe said the first time he met Carter as a 49er, he introduced himself and said, "I was on the BYU team that played you in the Holiday Bowl." Carter shook his finger at Holmoe and said, "We are never talking about that game. Do you understand me?"[6] Apparently, Carter did not believe that the game was a great moment in SMU football history. Jim McMahon said that whenever he has seen Eric Dickerson over the years, they jaw at each other a bit and Dickerson claims that BYU "stole" the game from SMU—that Matt Braga did not really make his controversial catch and so forth. McMahon explains, "I tell him that if he had just made the first down on that final SMU drive, the game was over!"[7]

History has amply illuminated just how talented the SMU team that played BYU in 1980 was. And not only because of the exploits of players like Dickerson, the NFL's single-season leading rusher of all time, and Carter, a three-time Super Bowl champion, who in 1984 would win both a Super Bowl ring and a silver medal in the shot put at the Olympic Games in Los Angeles. In 2010 ESPN sponsored a "30 for 30" documentary entitled "Pony Excess" (a pejorative twist on the SMU

Mustangs' nickname "Pony Express"). The film's description depicts a powerful SMU team:

"In the early 1980s, the Southern Methodist University (SMU) Mustangs were one of the best college football teams in the nation, riding high on the backs of Eric Dickerson [and] Craig James's celebrated 'Pony Express' backfield. Less than a decade later, the team would be shattered, rocked by the NCAA's first and only use of the 'death penalty' on a college football program.

"Twenty years later, director Thaddeus D. Matula, an SMU film school grad, chronicles the rise, fall, and rebirth of this once mighty program."[8]

The filmmaker points to the 1980 Holiday Bowl as both evidence of the rise of SMU as a football power in the late seventies and the beginning of the end for the Mustang dynasty—with the first NCAA sanctions coming down in 1981. When the NCAA issued the so-called "death penalty" for the SMU football program beginning in 1987, the sanctions were harsh and extensive. The 1987 football season was cancelled in its entirety; home games were cancelled for 1988; the number of coaches was limited; the program was banned from television and bowls games until 1989; scholarships and recruiting were severely limited; players were released from scholarships and allowed to attend other universities; and certain boosters were banned from the program. As a result of the penalties that were issued, the university also cancelled all other football games for the 1988 season.

The NCAA infractions report concluded: "The committee's penalties in this case are severe, and they are designed to compensate for the great competitive advantage Southern Methodist University has gained through long-term abuses and a pattern of purposeful violations of NCAA regulations."[9] SMU did not field a football team again until the 1989 season, starting from scratch.

The filmmaker refers to Holiday Bowl III as "possibly the greatest bowl comeback of all time." In the film several people affiliated with SMU football at the time more or less admit that the SMU teams of the early 1980s were "the best teams money could buy." One commentator said the joke among the SMU crowd was that Eric Dickerson—SMU's star tailback and future NFL leading rusher and Hall of Fame inductee—had to take a pay cut to go to the NFL. Dickerson laughs at the joke but does not deny most of the story—although he clarifies that he did make more money in his eleven-year NFL career.

Dickerson says that he will never, ever say what really happened to get him to sign at SMU.[10]

Dickerson had been the number one high school recruit in the country and, according to the film, was offered many gifts from several schools. He explains that Texas A&M offered his mother $50,000 cash in a brief-case, and other schools offered savings bonds, livestock, and other things. As chronicled in the film, Dickerson showed up for school one day with a new gold Pontiac Trans Am. The story that was circulated was that his grandmother bought it for him. Dickerson smiles and explains, "That's the story." The film makes it clear that many programs in the country were operating like SMU, but that SMU sort of set the standard. Dallas was flush with oil money and certain SMU boosters knew how to get the job done. At some level the feeling was that SMU had to mirror the same success the Dallas Cowboys were having in the NFL.

One SMU commentator, in justifying SMU's actions, points out that other teams cheated too. Then he argues, "At least SMU bought players who could play!" Prior to the death penalty, SMU was put on NCAA probation in 1981, with 29 recruiting violations, and again in 1985. In the meantime SMU won the championship of the powerful Southwest Conference in 1981, '82, and '84—with many of the same players who were underclassmen in 1980.

From 1981 to 1984, SMU had a 41-5-1 record—the best in the nation. That success was obtained with many players recruited by Ron Meyer and his staff in 1979, including Dickerson and James. Following the 1979 recruiting season, when SMU landed one of the best classes in the nation, famed football broadcaster Verne Lundquist said the question was, "How did they get these guys?" For his part Meyer insisted he didn't recruit players that would just be good college players; he recruited players who could play in the NFL.

From what I observed in San Diego in December 1980, he succeeded in reaching that goal. Perhaps SMU player Clement Fox summed it up best. He said he got so sick of hearing that SMU was the best team money could buy he would respond, "I played for SMU when we were paid to win and we did!"[11] Given the details about SMU recruiting violations advanced in "Pony Excess," and the consequent physical and athletic superiority of the SMU team, it is tempting to entertain the idea that the BYU victory in San Diego that night really was some kind of a football miracle.

The Race to San Diego
It was reported that SMU was not necessarily the first choice to be the visiting team for Holiday Bowl III. Early on, Stanford University was

picked as the odds-on favorite to play in the game. The press and bowl officials liked the idea of John Elway-led Stanford taking on Jim McMahon-led BYU. LSU, Navy, and Texas were also on the list of potential candidates. In the end, Stanford faltered late in the season, losing four of its final six games. Stanford also announced that due to final exam schedules it would not consider playing in a bowl game earlier than December 20, a day after the scheduled date for the Holiday Bowl. As a result, SMU, LSU, and Navy were identified as the final three, and on November 22 it was reported that the invitation had been extended to SMU. It all became official a few days later. The San Diego press was generally excited about the choice of SMU to play the WAC Champion.

For a period of time before BYU played Colorado State on November 15, there was some worry that CSU would beat BYU, win the WAC championship, and be the host team for the Holiday Bowl. Steve Bishoff, of the *San Diego Union*, wrote that "The Holiday Bowl doesn't need a Colorado State upset at Provo Saturday."[12] He noted that CSU was coming off a big win over UTEP 34–7. He said that seemed impressive until you remembered that BYU beat UTEP 83–7. In any event, there was no need to worry. Colorado State fell to the Cougars 45–14, behind a five TD pass effort from McMahon, who left the game for good with ten minutes left in the third quarter. As for the Mustangs, who finished the season with an 8-3 record and ranked in the top twenty, it was generally acknowledged in the press that SMU was the best visiting team to play in the young bowl game to that point.

Holiday Bowl III pitted the 11-1 and 14th ranked Cougars against the 8-3 and 18th ranked Mustangs. It was the first time that the Holiday Bowl featured two teams ranked in the top twenty. As in 1979 BYU again led the NCAA in total offense (535 yards per game), scoring (46.7 points per game), and passing offense (409.8 passing yards per game). SMU finished second in the powerful Southwest Conference, which included schools like Oklahoma, Texas, Arkansas, and Baylor. This made the Mustangs, even if they were ranked behind the Cougars in the polls, a one-point favorite over the WAC champions for the bowl game. BYU was a team that lived with a high-octane passing attack, led by their courageous all-American quarterback, Jim McMahon, who was the first Division I player to pass for more than 4,000 yards in a season—a threshold McMahon shattered with 4,571 yards in the 1980 season.

From left: Waldo Theus (66), Lott McIlhenny (40), Lee Spivey (76)

SMU was a smashmouth option running team-featuring future NFL stars Craig James and Eric Dickerson in the backfield—both were just sophomores in 1980—and many other players that commentators said looked as though they were ready for the NFL. BYU's captains for the 1980 season were Eric Lane and Nick Eyre from the offense and Glen Redd and Bill Schoepflin from the defense. These captains were outstanding leaders for the 1980 Cougars, and all four of them played in the NFL. The captains for SMU were center Lance Pederson and defensive back John Simmons, another future NFL player.

From the beginning, expectations were high for the 1980 Cougars. BYU received twenty-one of a possible twenty-four first place votes by coaches and writers prior to the opening of the WAC season. The way the voting was structured, the lower the total score, the stronger the prediction was for that team. For the 1980 vote, BYU scored twenty-seven total points. The next closest team was San Diego State University with sixty-four points and Utah was third with sixty-seven total points.

Much to the disappointment of the Cougars, to begin the 1980 season, BYU suffered a first-game loss against New Mexico in Albuquerque when the Lobos blitzed Jim McMahon on nearly every down. BYU linebacker Ed St. Pierre explained the loss in the *Salt Lake Tribune*: "They [New Mexico] had a lot of emotion and desire. We left our emotion and desire somewhere." St. Pierre also hinted that the loss to the Lobos would be a spark that could ignite the rest of the season for the Cougars. "Our pride is hurting. I'll tell you this; you'll be watching a new BYU team Saturday. I haven't seen this much fire and intensity since fall drills began. We've got something to prove." The loss to New Mexico haunted the team the rest of the season, but it also woke the team up. After that loss, we knew we could not take any team lightly for the rest of the regular season. And we didn't.

There was no margin for error following the New Mexico game. In order to repeat as WAC Champions, every game became a must-win. Most opponents were blown out, and McMahon and other starters were retired to the bench by the fourth quarter. Although McMahon started all twelve games, he only finished three of them, leaving ample playing time for his backups, Royce Bybee and Gym Kimball. McMahon missed the equivalent of two games of playing time during the season. That fact makes his 4500 passing yards and 47 touchdown passes an even more astounding accomplishment.

On December 16, 1980, three days before the bowl game, an NCAA Statistic Service Bulletin was issued, officially chronicling "the No. 1 season statistically of any quarterback *ever* in *any* NCAA football division." The bulletin stated that McMahon's record-breaking season had obliterated the passing efficiency and yardage marks set by Tulsa's Jerry Rhome after Rhome's remarkable season in 1964. The bulletin also pointed out how unlikely it is for a quarterback to lead in both yardage and efficiency—because those two statistics are mutually exclusive. If you have the type of passing game where you pile up a lot of yardage, you most likely won't be very efficient in that effort. The efficient passers are those who are throwing short passes.

For the season, BYU scored 560 points against 198 for its opponents. Along the way we beat Wisconsin in Madison (28 to 3) and Utah State in Logan (70 to 46). The Cougars also embarrassed the UTEP Miners in Provo 83 to 7. In that game, McMahon was sent to the bench in the third quarter with the score 49 to 7. He had thrown for 451 yards and six touchdowns. BYU threw no passes in the fourth quarter and Clay Brown showered and changed out of his game uniform at halftime. BYU scored three touchdowns in the fourth quarter by running the ball and on a pick-six interception return by defensive back Rob Wilson.

In an unsuccessful attempt to keep the score from getting completely out of hand, BYU emptied the bench early in the second half. Although I had played in the game as a back-up receiver and on the kickoff team, I was also inserted in the game in the fourth quarter as a defensive corner-back—a position I had not played since I was a sophomore in high school. I pointed this out to Coach Felt, the defensive backs coach, when he told me to go into the game as part of the defensive backfield, but I guess he figured a seventy-point cushion was enough to keep me out of trouble

Following tradition, the final game of the regular season—with the WAC Championship and Holiday Bowl invitation in the balance—was against arch-rival Utah. The game was in Salt Lake City, giving the Utes some optimism for an upset that would install them as conference champions and secure them a trip to San Diego for Holiday Bowl III. The sports headline for a John Mooney article in the *Salt Lake Tribune* for November 22, 1980, read "Utes entertain Cougars, hopes for holiday bowl."[13] On November 23, 1980, the Mooney headline said it all: "Cougars plaster Utes, 56-6, as McMahon leads march to WAC title and Holiday Bowl game."[14] Mooney had also penned a tribute to BYU, which proved prophetic for Utah and other WAC foes. He wrote, "It's easy to plan to fight the Cougar passing fire with fire, but against BYU a lot of teams have found themselves matchless."[15]

At the end of the regular season, the 1980 all-WAC team was announced and BYU had an astounding ten players on the first team. Jim McMahon, Clay Brown, Lloyd Jones, Nick Eyre, and Calvin Close were chosen for the offense. Glen Titensor, Brad Anae, Glen Redd, Bill Schoepflin, and Mark Brady were chosen for the defense. Brown was also chosen as the punter. McMahon was the only unanimous pick on the all-WAC team. BYU had come full circle from the New Mexico loss, and we were headed back to the Holiday Bowl in San Diego as WAC champions, still looking for the program's first bowl win.

BYU and SMU faced a common opponent in 1980: North Texas State. SMU played North Texas in Texas Stadium for the first game of the season and won 28 to 9. BYU played North Texas on November 8, 1980, and beat the Mean Green 41 to 23 in Provo. BYU jumped out to a 21–0 first quarter lead, but the Mean Green came back to make the game close at 24–17 before the Cougars were able to rally and put it away. In a post-game statement that was a preview of things to come for BYU with regard to teams from Texas, Coach Edwards stated, "North Texas State is as good as any team we've played this year." At the time Coach Edwards did not know that a few weeks later at the Holiday Bowl, he would face another Texas team that would be far superior to any team he had faced all year.

SIZING UP
THE ENEMY

We got our first look at the SMU team on
Wednesday of bowl week. The early indicator that we were
up against a formidable opponent was the eyeball test. We
were at the Town and Country Hotel for the Kiwanis Club–hosted kickoff luncheon at high noon. I can still see the SMU team walking into the
room for the luncheon. A San Diego sportswriter who witnessed the con-
vergence observed that when he stood next to the SMU and BYU players, it looked like the Dallas Cowboys against a college team—and we
weren't the Dallas Cowboys.[1] No one involved in the Holiday Bowl knew
anything about future NCAA penalties that would be levied against the
SMU team, but it was obvious that this team was different from our typical opponent.

The thing that impressed me most was the size and shape of their
interior linemen, on both offense and defense. We had some big players
on our team and some who were in very good shape and would go on to
play for years in the NFL. But, almost to a man, the Mustangs were huge,
ripped, and already looking like NFL players. I remember thinking as we
mingled with the SMU players during the week that it was clear football
training and lifting weights had been a much higher priority for them
than they had been for me. Although I was several years older than most
of them, due to a redshirt year and a two-year LDS mission, many of
them already seemed like pro players to me.

As it turned out, we arrived at the kickoff luncheon venue earlier than
SMU. When the Mustangs filed in the dining room, we were already

seated and waiting. (As I reflect on it, this was probably orchestrated by SMU for this very effect.) They were an impressive sight to see. I think at some level it startled many of us. There was sort of a hush in the room. It so happened that the NFL's San Diego Chargers were hosting the Pittsburgh Steelers the following Monday night in San Diego Stadium. Coach Edwards, who can always come up with a funny comment to break the tension, stood up, grabbed the microphone and said, "I'm sorry, you must have the wrong hotel. The Steelers' hotel is the next street over." Of course the place erupted with laughter, but the point remained: We knew from the moment we first saw them that we had our hands more than full with the Mustangs.

BYU's bowl history didn't ease the tension any. The school's 0-for-4 bowl record hung over the program like a plague. As menacing as SMU's physical stature was, the woeful bowl record was more menacing. Our frustration over the previous bowl losses was all but palpable. The week before the game, the *Denver Post* summarized the feeling very well with the headline, "Cougars must whip bowl hex or face credibility doubts."[2] The *Provo Daily Herald* asked "Can Cougars shake bowl jinx?"[3] Years later, Coach Edwards admitted that he had more anxiety about the 1980 bowl game than any of the other bowls, including the 1984 Holiday Bowl against Michigan—the game that gave BYU the national championship that year. Writing for the *Deseret News*, Lee Benson reported that, in comparing the preparation the team did for Holiday Bowl III to the preparation the team did for the Tangerine Bowl in 1976, Coach Edwards stated, "That . . . was when bowls were looked at like a reward. When they were fun and games. Now they're more like life and death."[4]

For all of his success at BYU—his phenomenal offensive firepower, all-American quarterbacks, WAC championships, and national attention—Coach Edwards had experienced nothing but frustration in bowl games. This fact overshadowed an otherwise remarkable makeover of the BYU program. Since he'd taken over as head coach in 1972, Coach Edwards' Cougar teams had won six conference championships and seventy-four games while losing just thirty. In the program's previous sixty-six years of existence, the record was 173-230 with just one conference title.

Prevailing wisdom in 1972 was that football and the private, church-owned school were somehow not compatible. In less than a decade, LaVell Edwards knocked that notion on its head. But still, there was the bowl issue. It wouldn't go away. Coach Edwards simply had to win the 1980 game. More than anyone, he was aware of it. At the kickoff luncheon, Coach joked, "I'm afraid my epitaph will be 'He Didn't Win a Bowl Game!'" Ray Scott shared this same sentiment with his national television audience when he observed, "LaVell Edwards has built one of the nation's fine football programs at Brigham Young but as he was kidding throughout the various official luncheons and dinners, and so forth, 'I don't want to be known as the coach who won a thousand games but never won a bowl game.'"[5]

Before our team left for San Diego in 1980, Rex E. Lee (former dean of the BYU law school and later BYU president), who was my LDS stake president at the time, told me to tell Coach Edwards that he knew BYU would win the game. He said it took him three trips to the United States Supreme Court as an advocate before he won one of those cases. He believed that Coach Edwards was going to match his record after three trips to the Holiday Bowl.

THE BYU
COACHES

BYU had an outstanding group of coaches and
support personnel during the 1980 season, many of whom went
on to find success in other programs. Sadly, three of the coaches
have passed away, all well before their time. Of course, Coach Edwards
stayed on at BYU until after the 2000 season and then retired as an
immensely beloved and successful coach. Edwards coached the 1984
National Champion Cougars. He coached a Heisman Trophy winner in
Ty Detmer, two Outland Trophy winners in Jason Buck and Mo Ele-
wonebi, and many all-American and NFL players—including one Hall
of Famer. LaVell Edwards is known as the visionary who brought the
unrelenting passing attack to college football. Some credit this style as the
inspiration, if not the model, for the so-called West Coast offense. Many
NFL teams have used this offense with great success, including the San
Francisco 49ers during the 70s, 80s, and 90s, when they won five Super
Bowls.

Coach Edwards developed a long and impressive list of all-American
quarterbacks, including two Super Bowl winners: Steve Young—who
was also the Super Bowl MVP—and Jim McMahon. Just before Coach
Edwards retired in 2000, Cougar Stadium was renamed LaVell Edwards
Stadium to honor the man and his legacy. Coach Edwards received his
own awards and honors along the way, including National Coach of the
Year. In 2004 he was inducted in the College Football Hall of Fame.
Coach Edwards was also a mentor to three young coaches who would
go on to be NFL head coaches and would take their teams to the Super

Bowl: Mike Holmgren with the Green Bay Packers and Seattle Seahawks, Brian Billick with the Baltimore Ravens, and Andy Reid (a lineman on the 1980 BYU team) with the Philadelphia Eagles.

When he retired after twenty-nine seasons, Coach Edwards's teams had amassed 257 victories. His teams won twenty conference championships and played in twenty-two bowl games. At the time he retired, he was the sixth winningest college football division one coach of all time. Given the program he was building at BYU, if it can ever be said that a coach "deserved" to win a game, Coach Edwards deserved to win a bowl game. But all that was future tense in 1980, when Coach was only in his ninth season at the helm of BYU football, He had just turned fifty years old a couple of months before Holiday Bowl III. After he retired from BYU, Coach Edwards and his wife Patti served a mission for the LDS Church in New York City. He remains active in many charitable causes and stays close to the BYU football program. Now, when he's asked if he plays much golf, he replies, "Only every day."[1]

BYU's offensive coordinator for the 1980 season was Doug Scovil, who was one of the many passing-game geniuses Coach Edwards brought in over the years as part of his strategy to make BYU a passing powerhouse. For the most part, the Cougar teams of the 70s, 80s and 90s lived up to that goal. Assistant coaches came and went, but the BYU passing attack was usually at the top of the college game and led the nation several times, including in 1979 and 1980—Doug Scovil's final two years at BYU. After the 1980 season and Holiday Bowl III, Scovil, who had also coached Roger Staubach at Navy, took the job of head coach at San Diego State University.

Coach Scovil could not duplicate the magic he had found and fostered at BYU with the Aztecs and finished after five seasons with a losing record. He then took a job as the quarterbacks coach for the Philadelphia Eagles, where he was credited with developing Randall Cunningham into a star NFL quarterback. Coach Scovil died of a heart attack in 1989 at the age of sixty-two after a workout at Veteran's Stadium in Philadelphia. There is no doubt that Coach Scovil was a significant factor in developing three of the key members of the BYU quarterback factory: Gifford Nielsen, Marc Wilson, and Jim McMahon. Scovil was the offensive mind behind the off-the-charts success BYU and Jim McMahon had offensively in 1980.

Norm Chow was the receivers' coach in 1980 and went on to coach for many more years at BYU as an offensive coordinator and as assistant head coach. He was there for many of the glory years of BYU football. He called offensive plays for the team during the 1984 championship season. Coach Chow went on to success in the college and pro ranks at places like North Carolina State, where he helped develop current NFL star Phillip Rivers as a quarterback; UCLA; USC, where he coached two Heisman Trophy winners in Carson Palmer and Matt Leinart; the University of Utah; and with the Tennessee Titans of the NFL. He is currently the head coach of the University of Hawaii. Coach Chow was my position coach at BYU and has remained a friend and a true gentleman all of these years. I was certainly not one of his star players, but he treats me like one whenever I see him.

Garth Hall was the running backs coach at BYU in 1980 and made his mark there, even though the focus of the offense at BYU was pass, pass, pass. Both of his starting running backs in 1980—Scott Phillips and Eric Lane—were drafted and played in the NFL. Hall was at BYU for nine seasons before leaving in 1981 to coach at Tulane University in New Orleans. He then became head coach at Idaho State University, where he stayed for four seasons. After a stint as an assistant at Oregon State University, he ended up as the last athletic director at Ricks College (now BYU–Idaho) in Rexburg, Idaho. Ricks had a very successful athletic program before intercollegiate athletics were cancelled at the college in 2000. Since then Coach Hall has remained as an administrator at BYU–Idaho and served as an LDS Mission President in Florida from 2010 to 2013.

Tom Ramage was the defensive line coach and he stayed at BYU and coached with LaVell Edwards for thirty years. He retired after the 2001 season. He coached two Outland Trophy winners in Merlin Olsen at Utah State and Jason Buck at BYU. His son John was on the 1980 BYU team and played a significant role on the kicking team that helped BYU with the fourth-quarter comeback in Holiday Bowl III.

Dick Felt was the defensive backs coach in 1980, which was his fourteenth season at BYU. He coached for many more years with Coach Edwards until 1993. Coach Felt, who had been a star in his own right at BYU, played seven years in the old AFL for the New York Titans and Boston Patriots. He was a two-time AFL all-star and helped the Patriots reach the 1963 AFL Championship game against the Chargers. As a result of his many years as a player, he had a great understanding of the game and could relate well with his players. In one game against San Jose State in 1952, he set a BYU record by scoring four touchdowns in one quarter. Almost fifty years to the day later, he passed away unexpectedly at age seventy-nine on a day that BYU was scheduled to play another football game against San Jose State. At his passing, the New England Patriots issued a press release stating that the Patriot's organization was "deeply saddened" to learn of his death.

Fred Whittingham was the linebackers coach and defensive coordinator for BYU in 1980. Fred was a bit of a legend in football circles long before he showed up at BYU. He had the nickname of "Mad Dog," acquired during his ten-year NFL career with the Rams, Eagles, and Saints. When I first met him, I remembered him from an NFL game years before when he got penalized for fighting. The announcers went on and on about what a tough guy Fred was and how he was not a person to mess with. That reputation followed him all the way to Provo. He was tough as nails as a coach but had learned to soften up a bit over the years and became a first-class gentleman and grandfather.

Perhaps Fred lived with such intensity because he felt he had cheated death once before and was possibly living on borrowed time. On October 29, 1960, Fred was in the hospital with a concussion and was unable to travel with his Cal-Poly football team. That day, the plane that the Cal-Poly team was flying in crashed, killing sixteen of his teammates. Fred was haunted by that memory for many years. Ted Tollner, who replaced Doug Scovil as offensive coordinator at BYU, and who later coached at San Diego State and USC, was on that Cal-Poly flight and survived the crash. That crash is often cited as one reason why former NFL coach and broadcaster John Madden refuses to fly—he had played at Cal-Poly just before the crash.

The players Whittingham coached would do anything for him in order to earn his respect, and he pushed players to make them great. They respected him for that approach. He coached his son Kyle as middle linebacker during the 1980 season. And as a father-and-son team, Fred and Kyle made critical calls and plays during the Holiday Bowl. Kyle was the leading tackler for BYU that night. Fred left BYU to coach in the NFL for the Rams and the Raiders before coaching at the University of Utah. There he hired Kyle to coach with him. Sadly, Fred died unexpectedly in 2003 following complications from surgery at the age of sixty-four.

Roger French was the BYU offensive line coach in 1980, his first year on the BYU staff. He had played in the NFL and coached in the Big Ten. He stayed with the BYU program until 2000 and left when Coach Edwards retired.

Mel Olson was an assistant coach for the offensive line and the junior varsity coach in 1980. Mel had played center and linebacker for BYU in the late 60s and earned all-WAC and honorable all-American honors as a center his senior season. He became part of the BYU coaching staff in 1970, shortly after his graduation, and coached and taught at BYU for many years.

Chuck Stiggins was the strength-and-conditioning coach. He was with the program for over twenty years and continues to coach and consult in strength and conditioning. Gary Zauner was the punting and place-kicking specialist. Zauner would go on to coach thirteen seasons in the NFL with the Cardinals, Ravens, and Vikings. Lance Reynolds, a former BYU football star and graduate assistant who would go on to coach on the Cougars staff until 2012, assisted with the offensive line. Kent Tingey, a former Cougar receiver, was a graduate assistant. Tingey obtained a doctorate degree and has been an executive administrator at Idaho State University for many years. Dave Smith, a former Cougar tight end, was also a graduate assistant.

Floyd Johnson was the equipment manager, a position he held for forty-six years. He passed away in 2002 at the age of eighty-three. Shirley Johnson was the football secretary, a position she held from 1980 until she retired in 2012. Doctors Brent Pratley and Wendell Gadd were team physicians, and Marv Roberson and Ollie Julkunen were the trainers. Marv passed away in 2010 and Ollie passed away in 2000. Glen Tuckett was the BYU athletic director. He held this position from 1976 to 1994, after a long and successful career as the BYU baseball coach, including being inducted into The College Baseball Hall of Fame.

Dr. Jeffrey R. Holland was BYU's newly appointed president in 1980, where he served until 1989, when he was called to serve as a general authority for the LDS church. He served in the First Quorum of the Seventy until 1994 when he was called to be a member of the Quorum of the Twelve Apostles, where he serves today.

THE RUN UP TO THE BOWL GAME

The 1980 BYU football team traveled to San Diego in two groups on December 14, 1980, on chartered Western Airlines flights. The coaches had decided to take the team to San Diego a day earlier than they had for the first two Holiday Bowl games in order to get in one more day of practice before the game. Although the weather caused flight delays getting out of Salt Lake City, by that evening everyone had arrived in San Diego. Team headquarters were at the San Diego Hilton Inn on beautiful Mission Bay, just north of the city.

The weather in San Diego was wonderful, especially after leaving the freezing cold winter inversion on the Wasatch front in Utah. Mission Bay and the Hilton were unbelievably beautiful and relaxing and almost other-worldly to those of us who were cramped in student housing in the snow in Provo, Utah.

The week was filled with many activities and diversions, but the primary focus was on team meetings and practice. After four prior bowl disappointments, including the first two heart-breaking Holiday Bowl losses, the coaches and team were focused on game preparation. Other distractions could not get in the way of preparations for the game, and we were reminded of that point multiple times every day. Practices were serious and intense.

Everyone seemed to be well aware that we had to win this game. The prospect of going 0 for 5 in bowl games was unacceptable for everyone. There was simply no room for defeat this time around. We did not come up with any special game plan for the Mustangs. We were number one in the nation in all major offensive categories, so the plan was to go with what we had been doing all year—with the exception of the New Mexico game. Rather than worry about our opponent, we would emphasize our strengths.

Several players recalled that much of our down time was spent in the Hilton pool playing water football. Wide receiver Scott Collie remembers spending so much time running in the pool that he raised blisters on his feet and he spent time on game night in the training room getting them drained and taped. Other than team meetings, practices, and official functions, we also spent time sleeping and watching television. Many players spent the bulk of their free time in the hotel game room.

One memory I have is running out to grab some fast food with fellow receiver Matt Braga in his truck and listening to the newly released Gaucho cassette from Steely Dan. Matt had driven his truck from Utah to the bowl game because he was planning to stay at his home in Southern California for the holiday break. I'm not sure why that memory has stayed with me all of these years, other than it was the first time I left the hotel and saw some sights around San Diego. I remember thinking it was amazing to be cruising around in warm weather with the windows down in late December.

During those early times in the week, we really had no idea how tough our Friday night test would be against the Pony Express. I've had several teammates ask something like: "Did we have any idea how good James and Dickerson were before the game?" I imagine the defense had some idea from watching the Pony Express on film to prepare for the game, but I don't think the rest of us knew what was about to hit us, especially early in the week.

On Monday we had free time in the morning and then practiced at San Diego State University (SDSU) in the afternoon. That evening we were treated to a buffet dinner at the hotel with the official athletic party and university administrators. On Tuesday we had team meetings in the morning and practice in the afternoon at SDSU. The Holiday Bowl Coronation Ball was that evening at the Holiday Inn Embarcadero. I'm not sure which team members attended that function, but most everyone I knew skipped it. Maybe some of us weren't even invited—I don't recall.

Tuesday evening after practice, I received a call from *Deseret News* sportswriter Brad Rock, whom I had known for years because we are from the same hometown of Rexburg, Idaho. He was in San Diego, staying in the team hotel and covering bowl week for the paper with fellow *Deseret News* sportswriter, Lee Benson. Brad said he was doing some research on what the players were doing in their free time and wanted to discuss it with me. One thing I told him was that we spent most of our time at the hotel because few of us had cars, and the Hilton was out on Mission Bay, several miles from downtown or other more populated areas. I guess Brad felt sorry for me because he asked if I would like to borrow his rental car. He said he would be in his room writing all night and had no use for it. I was happy to take advantage of Brad's generosity.

My roommate, quarterback Gym Kimball, and I waited until after we had dinner at the hotel and then we got the car keys from Rock and headed up I-5 to Los Angeles. A high school girlfriend of mine was attending USC, so we decided to visit her. Kimball wanted to see Sunset Boulevard so he took the car and disappeared while I toured some USC hangouts with my friend. My original plan was to visit my friend, see some sights around USC, and get back to the hotel by curfew. I think that was Kimball's plan too. My friend and I were back at her apartment at the agreed time but Gym did not show up. An hour or so later she got a call at her apartment from Kimball and I heard her ask him a few questions and then say, "Wow, you are lost!"

It took Gym the better part of another hour to find us and then we headed back to the Hilton in San Diego. We took a few more detours along the way and soon noticed that the sun was coming up about the time we reached Huntington Beach. We did not want to miss the opportunity to watch the sunrise so we walked out on the beach as the sun came up and illuminated the sand and ocean. It was breathtaking. We could not linger long because we were in danger of missing morning team meetings so we sped back down the freeway and made it to the hotel just in time for the meetings. Our teammates were puzzled as to why we were dressed in street clothes rather than sweats and shorts like most of them, but Kimball and I decided it would be best if we kept our all-night trip quiet. So much for not letting distractions get in the way of my game preparation.

On Wednesday we had team meetings in the morning before the luncheon at noon at the Town and Country Hotel—and our first look at SMU. NFL Hall-of-Fame receiver Lance Alworth was the featured speaker at the luncheon. BYU President Jeffery R. Holland also spoke and he shared some funny stories.[1] First, he drew a tongue-in-cheek comparison between the BYU football team and the Mormon Battalion that marched into San Diego in 1847 after a 1,900 mile march from Iowa during the Mexican-American War. He explained that when the battalion arrived in San Diego it was reported that they were "industrious," "respectable," and "highly favored." He said he wanted to put special emphasis on the "highly favored" point.

He also related a story about some Methodist preachers in England years ago, who complained to the police that the Mormons were preaching in the streets and something needed to be done about it. Brigham Young, who was a church leader in England at the time, got wind of the complaints and had the Mormons stay home. Thereafter, the police arrested a large group of street preachers and found out that they were all Methodists. Of course, with his now well-known timing and delivery, Elder Holland's humorous stories were very well received by the crowd.

Bill Orwig, a sports director for one of the San Diego area television stations, introduced Coach Edwards and jokingly said Coach was the most famous person in Utah after Donny and Marie. Once again, Coach got the last laugh by standing up and asking "Donny and Marie who?"

One other thing was interesting at the kick-off luncheon. In a pre-lunch press conference, Coach Meyer from SMU made comments about how he and Coach Edwards had known one another for years. He poignantly observed that Coach Edwards knew how to run a college football program the way it ought to be run.

Because we had a busy day on Wednesday, by the time we made it to practice in the afternoon, I was a near zombie due to the lack of sleep. Before practice began, McMahon was practicing his punting and was trying to see how much hang time he could get with his punts, and it was substantial. A few of the receivers were catching his punts. By that time in the day, my vision was blurry from lack of sleep and I was running very low on energy. As a result, McMahon's punts hit me everywhere but in the hands and I caught very few of them. When we finished and gathered as a team to begin practice, McMahon laughed and said, "I'm glad you're not returning punts on Friday." Since I was never a return man, there was no danger of me catching—or not catching—a punt, but his point was well taken. I was exhausted.

For some reason that I don't recall now, I spent a fair amount of practice time during the week running plays and drills as a scout team quarterback for our starting defenses—interception drills, corner drills, and so forth. I played a few positions for the JV team the year before, including reserve quarterback after Kimball broke his leg and had to sit out that year, so I was occasionally called on to step in as one of the prep team quarterbacks for the varsity in 1980. We had several quarterbacks with us in San Diego that week, so I don't recall why they used me at that position for our practices. But that day, after our all-night trip to LA, I was happy to be throwing and handing off the football rather than running endless pass routes as a receiver.

That evening, both teams were invited to a night at SeaWorld, which included dinner and tickets to the park and shows. Much of that evening is a blur to me, and I returned to the hotel early to rest and catch up on some much-needed sleep. I got to know one of the back-up quarterbacks for SMU that evening at SeaWorld, and he kept asking me if I would be willing to trade some of my BYU Holiday Bowl clothing and memorabilia after the game. We had been given cowboy hats, sweaters, shirts, jerseys, a commemorative wrist watch, and so forth, to add to our wardrobe for bowl week. The SMU player was very focused on making sure that he left San Diego with some BYU gear. I told him to meet me after the game and I would trade my BYU bowl sweater for his SMU sweater. Given the chaos and euphoria the ending of the game generated, I never saw the SMU player again—and made it back to Provo with my BYU sweater.

Kurt Gunther says it was at the SeaWorld event where he first noticed the size and shape of the SMU players, and he came away highly impressed.

On Thursday there was a Disneyland trip in the morning for families and the official team party and the usual team meetings for the rest of us. After the meetings, we left for the North Island Naval Air Station at Coronado Island. There we were treated to a tour of the USS Kitty Hawk (Aircraft Carrier C.V. 63). We toured the ship and had lunch on the hangar deck during a presentation of the Admiral's Trophy. Linebacker and Captain Glen Redd was presented with the Admiral's Trophy for BYU. Defensive lineman Harvey Armstrong was the recipient for SMU. The trophies were presented by VADM Robert F. Schultz, USN, Commander, Naval Air Force, US Pacific Fleet, with the inscription: "From the Navy team of professionals in honor of unselfish dedication, spirit and teamwork." Glen was certainly deserving of the honor for BYU, and the inscription was a spot-on description of him. The same can no doubt be said for Harvey Armstrong of SMU.

Among other activities, the starting offensive units for the teams posed for pictures for the press on the flight deck of the carrier. I recall thinking at the time that even though we'd had some jovial times with the Mustangs earlier in the week, people were starting to put on their game faces by the time we hit the deck of the carrier. Maybe it had something to do with the warrior mentality that the carrier and its crew exuded, but something in the wind started to change at that event. The fun was over and it was time to gear up for the bowl battle.

That evening we had a workout at the San Diego (Charger) Stadium as a final tune up for the game. We wore our game uniforms and spent an hour or so running through plays and getting used to the field. The stadium was decorated and ready to go for the game. It was an exhilarating night for all of us as we imagined a victorious outcome at the stadium the following evening. I'm sure that even those of us who would play little (if at all) in the game imagined great things happening to us the next night—including our first bowl victory. I knew that the game would be the final time I would put on a BYU Cougar uniform or, for that matter, a football uniform at all. After playing the game for well over a decade, I had some very mixed feelings that night. The last drill we ran was to set up the receivers and quarterbacks at midfield and have the receivers run fly patterns down the sidelines as the quarterbacks threw bombs into the end zone. We each caught several "touchdown" passes as we ended our final pregame workout. Maybe it was fortuitous that we ended with that drill, given the way things would develop at the end of the game the following evening.

Later that night we had our usual night-before-the-game cheeseburger and team meeting. Each night before games during that season, the team would gather together for cheeseburgers, watch inspirational game highlights, and go over assignments and game goals with the coaches. Then the coaches would leave the room, and the team would continue to meet together to talk about the game. Our goals for games during the 1980 season were usually something like 300 yards total offense, 200 yards passing and 100 yards rushing, 20 points scored, hold the opponent to 14 points, collect two turnovers, and commit no turnovers. (We exceeded these goals by a wide margin in nearly every game that season.)

That night and the following day, the team learned some important game lessons that we have never forgotten. Nearly every team member I have spoken to has mentioned one or more of these lessons and commented on how that game has continued to impact their lives for over thirty years.

GAME LESSON # 1
NEVER SAY "IMPOSSIBLE"

During these team-only sessions, the captains and the rest of the team would get one another pumped up with speeches or comments from the players, without the supervision or input of the coaches. Most of the time these meetings were, in fact, inspirational, but sometimes some of the speeches got out of control, and the team ended up laughing hysterically. Even those speeches helped loosen the team up before the games.

This particular team meeting became legendary in itself when our physically small but mentally tough and feisty team manager, Mel Farr, who had some health limitations, stood up in front of the team and announced he would tear the five-inch-thick San Diego telephone book in half with his bare hands. I can't recall specifically what I was thinking at the time, but I'm sure there were some doubters in the room. For much of the time, it looked like he would not be able to do it—and maybe not even survive. He was so determined to succeed that many of us worried he was going to have a stroke or something as the team cheered him on. McMahon stepped forward and tried to help, but Mel pushed Jim aside and gamely brushed off all other offers of help. I frankly thought we would have to call in for emergency medical help, it appeared to be that taxing for him. It took Mel many tense minutes to accomplish the task as the team shouted encouragement.

But, in the end, Mel succeeded and fell to the floor in an exhausted, sweaty heap alongside the torn telephone book. The team exploded with cheers and congratulations for Mel. We had just been shown an incredible demonstration of determination against long odds and never giving up. At the time, none of us realized the powerful omen his feat portended for the upcoming bowl game. It was the perfect overture for Holiday Bowl III.

In the video footage of the celebratory aftermath of the game, Mel can be seen jumping up on and hugging Coach Edwards in jubilation as Coach attempts to make his way across the field to shake hands with the SMU coach.

I don't know how much sleep anyone got that night. Everyone was too pumped for the game. We had an eleven o'clock curfew, but that

From left: Gym Kimball (11), Jim McMahon (9)

didn't mean any of us could go to sleep. Gym Kimball and I were in our room at about midnight watching TV and talking about the incredible week in San Diego when we heard a knock at our door. When I opened the door, there stood Jim McMahon. He simply said, "I can't sleep. Can I hang out in here?" I don't remember our room having a bed or curfew check; I don't think any of the coaches were terribly worried whether Kimball and I were getting the proper rest before the game. It was a little surprising, however, to see Jim McMahon wandering the halls of the hotel at midnight. We waved him in and stayed up until the wee hours of the morning shooting the breeze.

This episode at the Hilton in San Diego could not compare to one of McMahon's legendary stunts earlier in the year when the team was in Hawaii for a game against the Rainbow Warriors. There are several versions of McMahon's escapade in Hawaii floating around, but Matt Braga, who was Jim's travel roommate during the 1980 season, confirms that this is how the death-defying stunt went down.

Apparently, McMahon became bored in his hotel room on the twenty-fourth floor of the Waikiki Beach hotel and decided he was going to check and see if one of his teammates was in the room directly below his. Jim's roommate, Matt Braga, started to head out the door, and Jim said, "I'm going over the balcony." So over the balcony Jim went. Then he swung back and forth to get enough momentum to swing into the landing of the balcony below. Braga, who was afraid McMahon would fall to his death, tried to pull him up, but Jim waved him off and said, "I got it. I know my grip!"

When he swung in and landed on the balcony below, he found out it was a stranger's room, not one of his teammates, so he climbed back up the same way he had come down. The next day he looked over the balcony and declared, "Man, I can't believe I did that last night." His entry into our room in San Diego the night before the Holiday Bowl was not quite so dramatic.

Given the way the Holiday Bowl unfolded the following evening, I would give anything to have a recording of what we talked about that night, particularly what was on McMahon's mind the night before the SMU game. I do recall that Jim was aware of how important this game was to BYU and Coach Edwards—and, as the BYU quarterback, most of that weight fell on his shoulders. One hallmark of Jim's skill and success at the quarterback position was his ability to remain calm and rally his troops under pressure, as the Chicago Bears would learn a few years later.

He was his usual calm, humorous self, as I recall, but there was a slight edge to him that night. I think at some level he knew the monumental task that awaited him the following evening. As it is, all I have recorded from that night (early morning, rather) before the game is a picture I took of Gym and Jim in our hotel room, looking like they don't have a care in the world. One other thing I remember is that when McMahon finally left to go get a few hours of sleep, he simply said, "I better get some sleep before we go kick some [expletive]." His words would become prophetic, more or less—but not until the last few minutes of the game.

On Friday we had our pre-game breakfast at 9:30, followed by team meetings and some free time to hang around the hotel and get mentally prepared for the game. At two o'clock we had our pre-game dinner. Then we checked out of the hotel, boarded the buses, and left for the stadium. Game time was set for six o'clock.

I will never forget the feeling I had as we drove up to the stadium. The lights were on, the stadium was decorated, and the crowd was starting to gather. Mobile TV broadcast trucks were scattered around the stadium and parking lot. The whole scene was surreal for me. I could not believe we were in San Diego to play a post-season bowl game and that I was on that bus and part of that record-breaking BYU team after walking on to the team two years before.

41

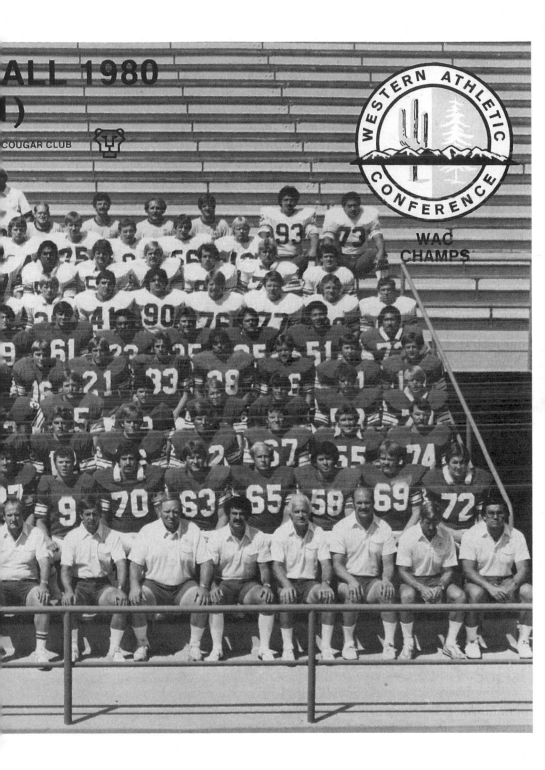

Brigham Young University vs Southern Methodist Universi

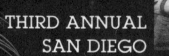

THIRD ANNUAL
SAN DIEGO

HOLIDAY
BOWL

December 19, 198
San Diego Stadiu

THE GAME

As has often been said, there were really two bowl games played that night in San Diego. The first game lasted for over three and a half quarters, during which time the Mustangs overwhelmed the Cougars. The second game lasted four minutes, during which time the Cougars overwhelmed the Mustangs. The NCAA official scoring summary for the game (see appendix) indicates that at kickoff time the temperature was sixty-four degrees. Kickoff occurred at 6:11 pm, and the game ended at 9:41 pm. The game was officiated by a team of officials from the Big Eight Conference. Little did they know the work they had ahead of them in a game full of spectacular, improbable plays that were hotly disputed. Some of those plays would be reviewed and debated for years. The game was played on natural grass, which was the first time SMU had been on grass all season. The National Anthem was sung by Grammy-winning singer Lou Rawls. Paid attendance was 50,214. Of the fifteen NCAA Division 1 post-season bowl games that year, the Holiday Bowl pay out was number nine, at $542,428.

The official game program for Holiday Bowl III ran a spotlight story on one of the senior leaders for each team. For SMU, it was all-American defensive back and punt-returner John Simmons. For BYU it was all-American tight end Clay Brown. The title for the Simmons spotlight was: "When SMU needs the Big Play."[1] The title for the Brown article was: "Clay Brown—The Complete Tight End."[2] It is eerie how those two storylines would intersect to dictate the outcome of the game. In the Simmons article, SMU head coach Ron Meyer is quoted as saying, "If I've got to win a game, my choice of any player on my team to do it would be John Simmons."[3] Unfortunately for Coach Meyer, at the end of this game, Simmons was on the bench, injured during the final play of the first half.

The Brown article makes the following point: "Subtract any of Clay Brown's passing or punting statistics from this year's BYU total, and the Cougar's success in 1980 just wouldn't be the same." The importance of his three touchdown effort, including the final "miracle" catch in the bowl game, cannot be overemphasized—not to mention his block on the final extra point kick.

One can only imagine how many times SMU Coach Ron Meyer has wished that he'd had his defensive star, John Simmons, on the field at the end of the game during the Hail Mary play. Certainly Brown would credibly argue that it wouldn't matter who was in there, he was not going to come down without that ball, but still, the question is there. Simmons was injured in sort of a freak fall on the last play of the first half—another BYU Hail Mary pass attempt of sorts from McMahon to Matt Braga. With six seconds left in the half, BYU obtained possession of the ball after an SMU punt. BYU ran a so-called "Waggle" play where McMahon appeared to be dropping straight back and then he sprinted toward the sideline where he launched a long pass downfield. McMahon threw the ball from BYU's nineteen yard line to the SMU nineteen—about the same distance he would throw the final Hail Mary pass to Brown. The pass was intended for Braga, who was streaking down the sideline. As McMahon let the ball go, Ray Scott exclaimed, "He's gonna let it all hang out!" Braga, Simmons, and a second SMU defensive back, Wes Hopkins, jumped for the ball. That time Simmons was there to make the play for SMU as time expired for the half. Simmons did not try to catch the ball; he simply batted it away for an incompletion.

However, in the process of batting the ball away, Simmons fell awkwardly on his arm, and in the game video, he can be seen writhing around on the field as the half ends. He dislocated his shoulder and did not play the rest of the game. The title of the Simmons article in the game program highlights the "what if" factor that comes into play in sports. After the game, the SMU defensive coach was reported as saying that the injury to Simmons caused the entire SMU defense to lose a certain amount of confidence in the second half. Even though Simmons was only one player, he was SMU's defensive leader. On the last BYU desperation Hail Mary or "Save the Game" play, as BYU called it at the time, SMU's leader was on the bench when Meyer needed someone to "win the game" for the Mustangs.

In fact, as BYU lined up for the final offensive play, Ray Scott reminded the audience that SMU had been playing without their "great" defensive back John Simmons since much earlier in the game.[4] Then again, for three and a half quarters, the Mustang defense—with or without John Simmons—had had no difficulty holding BYU's offense in check. As I've said, I frankly think that part of the story of BYU's three-quarter-long funk might have been that BYU came into the game a little overwhelmed by the Mustangs. All of those joint appearances alongside the impressive-looking Mustangs at bowl week functions had struck a subtle psychological blow.

With only five minutes elapsed in the game, and the score already 16–0 for SMU, color announcer Grady Alderman, the former Minnesota Viking great, queried, "One wonders if this BYU team isn't just a little bit nervous. Even though this is their third consecutive Holiday Bowl, they appear to be having great difficulty putting anything together." Later, in the second quarter, he would echo that same comment and say, "One wonders if BYU— the players—aren't getting just a little bit frustrated: unable to do anything on offense and really unable to contain this SMU offense, as well."[5]

After the game, Coach Edwards admitted that his starters had been tight in the first half, but he couldn't come up with a good explanation for it. He had thought his team was ready to play the game. BYU middle linebacker Kyle Whittingham observed, "We played like we were in a trance in that first half." SMU's running back Craig James agreed, "I thought BYU was a little intimidated to begin with."[6] No one can be certain why teams show up flat for games, but there is no question BYU came out flat in the 1980 Holiday Bowl. I suspect those first couple of meetings with the Mustangs, along with the pressure to finally win a bowl game, may have had a little something to do with it.

I'm not saying that our team was scared or consciously intimidated at all. Far from it. Following the opening loss to New Mexico, we had been a football juggernaut the rest of the season—and maybe even had too much confidence going into the bowl game. But I do believe that subconsciously, the size and physicality of the Mustangs eroded that confidence in a way that none of us recognized until after the opening kick-off.

Neither team could do much with their early possessions. "We've played just about two minutes and we have no score," announced Ray Scott. On the very next play, Eric Dickerson sprinted around the corner for SMU's first touchdown from the BYU fifteen. SMU was off to the races. It would soon be 19 to 0 for SMU. It seemed like every few plays, Eric Dickerson or Craig James—SMU's other future NFL back—were sprinting past our defense into the end zone or for long gains, including a fake punt that James ran in for a touchdown. Dickerson even did a sort of vault/somersault like Superman over our defense and into the end zone for one touchdown. Scott called it a "spectacular" touchdown.

Although I don't know if any of us realized we were watching and playing against a runner who would become one of the greatest running backs in NFL history and an NFL Hall of Famer, we did know he had a special set of skills. He was big and very, very fast. Then BYU Athletic Director, Glen Tuckett, said that when he saw Dickerson warming up before the game his thought was, "This could be a very long night."

Dickerson scored two touchdowns, and James scored three—including his run on the fake punt. Following Dickerson's first touchdown, Grady Alderman exclaimed, "I'm not sure BYU is ready for all of this speed." The Mustangs were marching up and down the field, almost at will. Their freshman quarterback, Lance McIlhenny, ran their option to near perfection. Dickerson and James were having a spectacular game, but McIlhenny was clearly their inspirational leader on offense.

McIlhenny had not begun the season as the starter for SMU, but he was promoted in their seventh game against the University of Texas in Austin. SMU defeated Texas 20–6. In that game McIlhenny guided SMU to 283 yards on the ground and the "Pony Express" was born. We had faced some good option teams during the season, but none that came anywhere close to the Pony Express and their trigger man, McIlhenny.

On the BYU side of the ball, we had trouble sustaining a drive. The first two drives, McMahon was nearly intercepted twice. BYU went punt, punt, punt/safety on the first three drives. BYU guard Calvin Close said he realized on the first play that the SMU defensive tackle he was facing was much more powerful than anyone he had lined up across from, not just that season, but in his three seasons at BYU. "We knew from the first play that we really had our hands full with SMU," Calvin recalled. Calvin played the game with a strap connecting the back of his helmet to the back of his shoulder pads. The strap was designed to alleviate pain that he was experiencing from a pinched nerve in his neck that had bothered him all season. When I asked Calvin why they used the strap, he replied, "Because they couldn't figure out how to attach my head with a screw!" He was only kidding, I think.

Offensive guard Lloyd Eldredge had a similar experience. Early in the game, SMU defensive lineman Harvey Armstrong hit Lloyd so hard it gave him a mild concussion—really rang his bell. Lloyd said he had never played against anyone who hit so hard and was so strong. It is a tremendous credit to these BYU linemen that they kept firing away at the powerful SMU defensive line throughout the game, even though the game took a heavy physical toll on the BYU players.

Near the end of the first quarter, Ray Scott made the following observation: "So, with 4:21 left to play in the first quarter, Southern Methodist University has stunned the Cougars. I don't think anyone expected what we have seen so far here in this third annual Holiday Bowl—[that] the high-scoring Cougars would be held scoreless with 4:21 left to play in the first quarter, that Jim McMahon would so far be unable to complete a pass, that the Cougars would be without a first down and that the Mustangs would be leading 19–0, but that is what we have seen."

Late in the first quarter, BYU finally scored on a long touchdown pass from McMahon to Brown. Brown caught the ball with his left hand by trapping it against his hip, and then he turned to sprint sixty yards, outrunning the SMU defense to the end zone, with receiver Dan Plater escorting him down the field. It was an amazing play, especially when you consider the ineffectiveness the BYU offense had shown up to that point.

From left: Vai Sikahema (23), Scott Pettis (29)

GAME LESSON #2

SOMETIMES WHEN THINGS LOOK
HOPELESS, TAKE A RISK AND RUN LIKE YOU
HAVE NOTHING TO LOSE

BYU scored again near the end of the first half on an 83-yard punt return by freshman Vai Sikahema. In a reversal of fortune from the 1979 Holiday Bowl, Sikahema did nearly the same thing to SMU that Tim Wilbur of Indiana had done to BYU.

The SMU punt was not as long as Vai had anticipated. Vai hung back as though he would simply let the punt bounce so the ball could be downed by the Mustangs. SMU noticed what Vai was doing, so they eased up a little in their pursuit and began to settle down around the ball. At that point, Vai made a split-second mental calculation and decided that given the score and the point in the game, he didn't have anything to lose. Just as SMU geared down, the ball bounced in Vai's direction. He grabbed it and, already running toward the other end zone, he turned on the speed, threw a couple of moves on SMU defenders, and sprinted nearly untouched to the end zone at the other end of the field.

It was a spectacular, gutsy play by a freshmen return specialist—one that coaches would not necessarily encourage or teach. But it was a critical play for BYU in the Miracle Bowl, preventing the game from becoming a complete blowout in the first half. McMahon recalls grabbing Vai after the punt return and telling him, "Kid, you have just given us a chance!" It would get worse before it got better for BYU, but McMahon had a point.

In the first quarter, Sikahema had been leveled by a ferocious hit by SMU's Waldo Theus on one kickoff return. Shortly thereafter, on an SMU punt, Sikahema fumbled but was able to fall on the ball and retain possession for BYU. BYU was lucky on that fumble as the first player to reach the ball was an SMU player who was moving so fast he sort of slid off the ball and allowed Vai to recover it. Had SMU recovered that fumble very close to the BYU goal line so early in the game, that would have compounded the first-half disaster.

The memory of those two unsuccessful earlier returns conditioned Sikahema to take a chance on the punt—he is not one to go away quietly. Regardless, it was a huge play for the Cougars going into the second half.

The BYU defense also made some plays in the first half. SMU had to punt a couple of times, one of which obviously gave Sikahema his chance, and there were other key stops. The BYU defense made many swarming tackles during the game, which shows that they were slugging it out every step of the way—if, at times, with limited success against the Pony Express.

GAME LESSON #3

TEST THE OPPOSITION'S VULNERABILITIES

AND THEN EXPLOIT THEM

One of my favorite defensive plays of the game was a tackle Bill Schoepflin made on SMU receiver Mitchell Bennett at the beginning of the second quarter. The game announcers had identified Bennett as a threat for SMU with his exceptional speed and ability to run reverses. As SMU approached the goal line, Bennett caught a pass over the middle from McIlhenny. Schoepflin, who had been a three-year varsity wrestler at Arvada High School in Colorado, grabbed Bennett and threw him to the turf with a wrestler's move that made Bennett look like a rag doll. He almost bounced!

Bennett jumped up and angrily threw the ball at Schoepflin. Schoepflin immediately returned the favor and threw it back at Bennett. As usually happens in those situations, the second player got hit with the penalty. Schoepflin was whistled for unsportsmanlike conduct, and SMU went on to score. But that was the only pass Bennett caught in the game, and he was not much of a factor the rest of the evening. In fact, on what would be the last offensive play SMU ran, SMU faced a third down and eight situation. The Mustangs ran Eric Dickerson on a sweep to the left. Bennett was sent in motion to the left to be the lead blocker for Dickerson Schoepflin easily brushed off Bennett and tackled Dickerson after a yard and a half gain, forcing SMU to punt. Schoepflin then blocked the punt and put the ball back in McMahon's hands to set up the miracle Hail Mary. If Bennett had made the block on Schoepflin, Dickerson would have made the first down, and SMU could have simply run out the clock on BYU and won the game. McMahon would have had no chance to pull off the Hail Mary miracle.

I'm convinced that Schoepflin's manhandling of Bennett on that pass reception in the first half came into play on SMU's final offensive play as Dickerson attempted to gain the game-ending first down. Bennett's block on Schoepflin never really materialized, and Schoepflin stopped Dickerson cold after Dickerson was slowed up briefly by Tom Holmoe.

At the half the score was 29–13 for the Mustangs, but the game was

From left: Glen Titensor (76), Tom Holmoe (46), Kyle Whittingham (59)

not really that close. There wasn't much to indicate the BYU onslaught that would come later in the second half. There was this: with seventeen seconds to play in the half, SMU was forced to punt. Ray Scott and Grady Alderman wondered briefly whether BYU would try to block the punt or drop everyone back and go for a well-blocked return. They concluded that BYU was not going for the block. But as the play commenced, they could see that Bill Schoepflin charged the punter from the BYU left, and Scott declared, "Oh, they did go for it and Schoepflin almost got one!" As Alderman and Scott had noticed, Schoepflin came within a few inches of blocking that punt. SMU's coaches would have done well if they'd paid closer attention to Schoepflin's first-half block attempt and plugged up that hole before the end of the game. Schoepflin did pay attention to that play, and he filed that information away to be used in the final, crucial minute of the game.

The halftime entertainment included performances by the marching bands from SMU, BYU, and San Diego State University (SDSU had made it to the Holiday Bowl after all). Chris Brown, representing Holiday Inn, which was a sponsor of the game, was interviewed by Duane Dow of the Mizlou TV Network. Even though things looked very bleak for BYU at the half, Brown predicted the outcome of the game when he declared,

"I think it's going to be a good game, and I think BYU is going to come back." He was one of a few who were willing to predict the BYU comeback at that point. One other believer was Tammy Garrett from Glendale, California, who would later marry BYU offensive lineman Andy Reid. Tammy, who was dating Andy at the time, had been invited to sit with Andy's mother high in the stadium (where many of the player's seats were located). In the fourth quarter, as the mass exodus from the stadium began, Tammy recalls standing up and shouting at the fans who were leaving, "You're gonna regret it when we come back and WIN!" It turns out that she was spot-on in her prediction, but at the time she was worried that Andy's mother might think she was a little crazy.

I wish I could tell you what occurred in the locker room at halftime but I have no memory of anything that went on during the break. Usually we would meet with our position coaches and then come together with Coach Edwards before we returned to the field. Even though Coach Edwards is a great and articulate speaker, he was not usually one to get all wound up at halftime and deliver a rousing speech. Typically, in his understated way, Coach would offer words of direction and encouragement. No one that I have talked to remembers much of anything about our halftime break. You would think some of the coaches would have been breathing fire in the locker room, given the way the game was going for us, but no one recalls much of anything. Maybe we did get berated and yelled at but those memories were all obliterated by the ending of the game. Defensive back Mark Brady recalled vaguely that Coach Felt was pretty worked up and challenged his players to have some pride and play with more heart in the second half. Beyond that, our memories have faded.

The carnage continued in the third quarter, which ended with SMU's dominance still unchallenged. SMU scored on the one-yard leap by Dickerson to make the score 35 to 13 and then midway through the quarter, Clay Brown scored his second touchdown of the night on a 13-yard pass from McMahon. Both teams attempted to score two-point conversions but failed in those attempts. SMU kicked a 42-yard field goal to finish out the quarter, with a 38–19 lead. Early in the fourth quarter, the television cameras began showing sideline shots of the SMU players mugging for the cameras and prematurely celebrating a victory. "A very happy group of Mustangs, and they smell a victory," exclaimed Ray Scott, who then added, "But we still have eleven minutes to play!"[7]

GAME LESSON # 4
NEVER, NEVER,
NEVER GIVE UP

With about eight minutes remaining, BYU faced a fourth and two situation on its own forty-six yard line. Coach Scovil told Coach Edwards that BYU should punt. BYU sent the punting unit into the game, but McMahon refused to come off of the field. He was livid. The coaches tried to wave him off the field, and the punt team sort of milled around, unsure of what they should do. Finally McMahon turned toward the coaches on the sideline and, with a stream of expletives, screamed "Are we just going to give up!?"

The coaches quickly called a timeout, and after a heated discussion, it was determined to call off the punting team and go for the first down. It is great to watch that play. There is just no doubt in McMahon's body language that he knows the play will succeed. Even television viewers who watch the footage comment about the look in McMahon's eye. His resolve galvanized the team and is a great example of how important his leadership was to the team. Calling out the play as an audible from the line of scrimmage, McMahon hit Brown on a five yard out, which Brown stretched into a twelve-yard gain for a first down. When Coach Edwards now explains the decision to go for the first down and the heated exchange with McMahon, he jokingly says that McMahon stormed off the field and yelled "Golly gee whiz, are we really going to punt? I don't like that idea!" Understanding the import of that play to BYU, and echoing what Jim McMahon sensed at the time, Grady Alderman explained: "If they were serious about winning this game, they had to go for that first down." After BYU gained the first down, McMahon marched the

Jim McMahon (9)

offense down the field to the goal line, where Scott Phillips scored on a one-yard dive into the end zone, bringing the score to a respectable 38–25.

It is interesting that McMahon claims Sikahema's punt return was when the momentum shifted, and Sikahema claims that McMahon's defiance of the coaches on the punt call is when the momentum shifted. In reality the momentum ebbed and flowed well into the fourth quarter.

If you had to pick a play where the momentum shifted to BYU and the comeback really began, that fourth down play would be a prime candidate—even though SMU quickly answered with another touchdown that appeared to be the proverbial nail in BYU's coffin. There was just no quit in McMahon, and his colorful refusal to accept the decision to punt began to turn the tide of the game.

After the Phillips score and an unsuccessful try for a two-point conversion, BYU attempted an onside kick. Freshman kicker, Lee Johnson, tried the onside kick but he hit the ball too high and after one bounce the ball popped straight up and grazed him after it had only traveled about three yards. As a result, the kick became a dead ball, and SMU got the ball back in great field position on the BYU forty-two yard line. On the next play, SMU ran a sweep around the right side with Craig James carrying the ball. The BYU defense closed off the right side and, for a moment, it appeared as though James would not advance very far. Just then, James saw an opening to his left, so he quickly reversed field with nothing but open field on the left side. He sprinted forty-two yards for another SMU touchdown.

The extra point was good and the score stood at 45–25 with 3:57 left to play. That is when many in the stadium and watching on television called it a day, including Ray Scott. The announcer informed his TV audience, "So that just about puts the icing on the cake. . . . SMU has put 45 points on the board. And for Brigham Young, it turns out to be its third fruitless trip to the Holiday Bowl."[8] Scott's comment certainly did not seem unreasonable at the time. That touchdown was particularly discouraging to our team, and many heads hung in frustration. The momentum shift in BYU's favor appeared to vaporize as James sprinted into the BYU end zone. It was extremely demoralizing when it looked like the defense had swarmed to shut down James, only to have him reverse field and run over forty yards for another SMU score.

GAME LESSON # 5
SOMETIMES SUCCESS COMES IF YOU DIVE
AT A PROBLEM AND HANG ON UNTIL
THE DUST CLEARS

Coach Edwards recalls it was about at that point when the thought briefly popped into his head that he hoped he didn't have to come back to that bowl game again. I recall walking over to Royce Bybee, McMahon's backup; and assuming that the teams would soon start clearing their benches, I said, sort of tongue-in-cheek, "We'll probably get to play now." Royce laughed at the gallows humor. Phillips remembers that he leaned over to Dan Plater and said something to the effect of, "Man, it's happening to us again." Plater recalls that when he missed a two-point conversion pass from McMahon in the third quarter, his first thought was, "Big deal. There is no way we can catch them anyway. They're killing us." McMahon says he was livid because he "had stunk it up in the first half, and the defense couldn't stop them." It was not a pretty picture on our sideline. The exodus from the stadium, already underway since just before the fourth quarter began, picked up in speed and intensity. Even Clay Brown's mother left the game to begin the two-hour drive home. Little did any of the people leaving, or most of us who were there to stay, realize what would happen in the next four amazing minutes.

Following the SMU kickoff, BYU marched down the field and McMahon, on a broken play where he had to scramble out of trouble, connected on a fifteen-yard pass to Matt Braga diving in the end zone. There was no immediate touchdown signal. The game officials appeared to be confused about what call to make. Finally after looking at each other for a few seconds and then at Braga, one of them signaled a touchdown. Because they did not see a skip of the ball and Braga had the ball in his hands when he jumped up dramatically at the end of the play, the refs made the call in Braga's favor. They clearly took Matt's dramatics with the ball in his hand as evidence that he caught it. Six points Cougars: SMU 45, BYU 31.

One of the SMU defensive backs covering Braga, Reggie Phillips, threw a fit and complained loudly that the ball had hit the ground before Braga grabbed it while sliding and rolling along the end zone turf. From my vantage point, there was no obvious skip of the ball on the turf. This was long before official video review of such plays, but even if there had been a review, the replay was inconclusive and would not have resulted in the call being changed. Moreover, the SMU defensive back was in no position to see the play any better than the rest of us. He dove in front of Braga, so his back was turned to the play and the ball and he couldn't see what happened either.

When Matt came off of the field I asked him if he had caught it. Seeing the fit the SMU player was still throwing for the referee, he shrugged and said, "I don't know, maybe it bounced." Later, when we watched the game film, we could see that the ball initially hit Braga's forearm, then flipped up and hit his shoulder pad before it settled into his arms as he slid along the turf, rolled over and jumped up with the ball in his hand. It is not clear whether it hit the ground through that process or not. After we saw the replay, Braga agreed that it looked like it was a catch.

Coach Edwards reported that Matt told him he wasn't sure if he caught it—again, in part, because of how strongly the SMU defender protested. Braga explained that he knew the ball hit his arm first and then flipped up to his chest but he is not certain what happened after that, before the ball ended up in his hands. Matt said, "It looked like I was making the touchdown sign with my arms when I jumped up, but I was really just as surprised as everyone else that the ball ended up in my hands and I was showing that surprise by hoisting the ball."

Because of the way he dove for the ball while running at full speed and then sliding along the ground, it is not surprising or contradictory that Matt really doesn't know what happened. Given the speed at which the play unfolded, just because Braga initially wasn't sure if he caught it does not mean it was not a catch. When you are sliding along the ground at full speed, you don't have the luxury of frame-by-frame slow motion, and it is nearly impossible to keep track of every little nuance of those few seconds on the ground. It is just as likely that the ball never did touch the turf but was cradled by Braga as he slid and rolled along the turf—otherwise how would he have rolled up and out of his slide with the ball firmly in his hands? Even announcer Grady Alderman could see what happened. In describing the play to the television audience he explained, "He got his right hand underneath it and flips it up to his chest and hangs on."

The call was debated in the press and was even referred to as a "phantom" catch by one writer.[9] In a funny twist to this story, the *Provo Daily Herald*[10] weighed in on the debate and claimed it had irrefutable proof that Braga caught the pass. The paper ran a picture that it claimed was Braga catching the pass. Unfortunately, the picture is of Cougar wide receiver Bill Davis catching a pass while sliding on his knees earlier in the game.[11]

In another ironic episode regarding Braga's touchdown catch, Cougar running back Scott Phillips recalls getting taken to task by an irate Cougar fan on a radio call-in show a few days after the game because the fan thought that Phillips had been disloyal to the team and Cougar nation by saying that Braga did not catch the TD pass. Scott Phillips recalls that he was quoted in a local paper as saying he saw the ball hit the turf first. Once again the press got it about half right. *Scott* Phillips never said such a thing at all, as it was reported in the paper. SMU defensive back *Reginald* Phillips, who was covering Braga on the play, in fact, made that claim. He was the SMU defensive back who threw the tantrum after the touchdown was called. Apparently the reporter only heard the Phillips part and assumed it was Scott Phillips. I guess we all know what happens when you assume things.[12]

Braga gives partial credit for his diving touchdown catch to a drill we came up with a few weeks before in November as we were preparing to play the University of Utah. The weather in Provo was poor, so we had a couple of practices at the indoor turf facility in the Smith Fieldhouse on the BYU campus. There was limited space in that facility at the time so we had to get creative with our drills. The BYU track team had set up their high jump and long jump pits in the practice facility with foam pads in the pits to cushion their falls. Braga explains, "It was your idea that we had balls thrown to us as we dove into the pit to practice making diving catches. Who knows, without that practice maybe I don't come up with the diving catch against SMU and we don't score."[13]

Cosmo (00)

GAME LESSON #6
LEARN TO TRUST YOURSELF

The Cougars immediately got the ball back by recovering kicker Lee Johnson's second attempt at an onside kick. Johnson explains that there was some drama on the sideline before he took the field and made the kick. Because his first attempted onside kick was such an unmitigated disaster, Lee had zero interest in attempting another one. When the special teams coach, Gary Zauner, told Johnson to try a second onside kick, Johnson queried, "Are you sure?" Zauner confirmed that was exactly what he wanted. Johnson jokingly explains, "At that point, I was just a scared freshman and all I wanted to do was go home and cuddle with my blankie. I was demoralized after that first failed onside kick and had no desire to try it again." Lee then suggested to Zauner, "Maybe you should have somebody else do it."[14] That did not go over well with Coach Zauner, who told Johnson in no uncertain terms to get his backside out on the field and make the kick. To Lee's credit, his second attempt was near perfect. Tom Holmoe, with an assist from freshman Todd Shell, recovered the ball for BYU. There is still a bit of a disagreement between Tom and Todd about who actually recovered it. Not to worry—they've only been debating it for nearly thirty-five years. I'm sure they will figure it out at some point.

Following the onside kick, McMahon connected on a long pass to receiver Bill Davis, where it appeared that Davis broke the plane of the end zone with the ball. BYU had reason to complain about that call because from the replay it seems clear that Davis was knocked out of bounds with the ball on the end zone side of the pylon. Ray Scott called it a touchdown from his vantage point in the press box. The refs didn't see it that way and spotted the ball on the one-foot line. Even though BYU scored on the next play, we still lost some precious seconds with that call. Davis was sure he scored, so the refs made some calls that were disputed by both teams. There was certainly no guarantee that BYU would score on the next play, so it was an important call that could have determined the outcome of the game—and the refs called it SMU's way.

In another twist of fate, McMahon had called an audible on the play so Davis was not supposed to have been running that deep route anyway.

Bart Oates (50), Bill Davis (88), Cosmo (00)

Davis did not hear the audible from his split receiver position. After the snap of the football, it appears from the game tape that McMahon is looking for Davis on a quick-out route, but seeing that Davis was running a deep corner route instead, McMahon had to scramble a bit to get an opening to throw a deeper ball. That hitch-up where McMahon briefly set to throw a quick-out pass may have been just the diversion that was needed for Davis to get behind the SMU defenders.

Luckily McMahon saw Davis and got the ball to him just before Davis reached the goal line, forty yards away. Without that long play, BYU would have likely burned up many more precious seconds covering that same distance. That was a lucky, unplanned, and inexplicable play that was a huge contribution to the comeback. If Davis had run the correct quick-out pattern, at best, BYU might have made a ten-yard gain. Instead BYU got the ball on the one-foot line with just over two minutes to play. McMahon missed the drama of the play at the goal line because he was leveled by SMU defender Richard Neeley just as he let the pass fly.

Cougar tailback Scott Phillips sprinted past the Mustang defense into the end zone for the score and then caught a pass from McMahon for the two-point conversion. SMU 45, BYU 39. In explaining his touchdown, Phillips recalled that the play was called as a halfback pass, not a run. In watching the replay, it's clear that Phillips is only running about half speed as he leaves the backfield after taking the handoff from McMahon. I wondered for years why Phillips was only jogging as he took the handoff on the play. Going half speed was not his style. Phillips explained that he was looking for someone to throw the ball to. Because he could see that he had a clear path to the end zone, he decided to outrun the SMU defense for the score, rather than take a chance on a pass. Phillips was one of the fastest sprinters on the 1980 team, so he knew he had better odds just running the ball in. He turned on the jets and sprinted around the corner into the end zone untouched. Phillips said, "That just shows you how Coach Scovil's pass-happy mind worked. We're on the one-foot line and he wanted to throw a halfback pass. It was unbelievable."[15]

After the two-point conversion, Ray Scott amended his earlier prediction of an SMU victory and declared, "Don't go away, folks!" Unfortunately Scott's advisory was too late for many people who had either left the stadium or had turned off their television sets and gone to bed. The Cougars tried another onside kick, which Johnson executed well, but the Mustangs recovered the ball at midfield.

The fired-up Cougar defense stopped the Mustangs from gaining a first down. First, Kyle Whittingham led a swarm of defenders that stopped Dickerson for no gain up the middle. On the next play, it appeared that McIlhenny was looking to throw the ball before tucking it in and running with it. Glen Redd quickly stopped McIlhenny for about a two-yard gain. On third down, with eight yards to go for a first down, Bill Schoepflin brushed off Bennett's attempted block and tackled Dickerson after a yard gain on a sweep, and the Mustangs had to punt. SMU ran the clock down to take away as much time as possible and received a delay of game penalty, moving the ball back five yards. Both Ray Scott and Grady Alderman expressed serious reservations that SMU should punt at all.

SMU attempted the punt, but Bill Schoepflin, who had nearly blocked the SMU punt at the end of the first half, employed the same slashing and diving technique and squarely smothered the football with his body just as it left the kicker's foot. It gave the Cougars the ball on the SMU 41 yard line with thirteen seconds to play. BYU had no time-outs remaining. Sikahema recalls that in the huddle for the punt return, Schoepflin said, "I'm going to get this one."

McMahon threw two incomplete passes, one attempt to Brown over the middle and a bomb down the sidelines to Lloyd Jones, leaving the Cougars still 41 yards from pay dirt with just three seconds remaining. It was only third down, but there was only time left for one last, desperate play.

Radio announcer Tony Roberts and his companions said it best, "Three seconds left to go. This is it. This is it, indeed. 84 points on the scoreboard. 45 to 39. . . ."

GAME LESSON # 7

WANT IT MORE THAN THOSE

TRYING TO STOP YOU

BYU coaches called the "Save the Game" play. McMahon ordered the linemen to give him some time and told the receivers to get to the end zone. Scott Phillips recalls that the call was for both backs to stay put in the backfield and block for McMahon. McMahon ordered, "I'm going to throw it in the end zone, so somebody better catch it. We came too far to lose this game." Brown, the tight end, was to run down the middle of the field, and the two wide receivers, Dan Plater and Bill Davis, were to sprint down the sides as wingmen—they were supposed to be on alert for a tipped ball. The Save the Game play was in our playbook. We would occasionally run it at the end of practice as a way to put some fun into the drudgery of post practice conditioning. Little did we know that the play would finally put the Cougars within an extra point kick of a bowl victory and keep BYU in the discussion about the most exciting bowl games ever for thirty years and counting.

The play was designed to get an interference call or a tipped ball that could be caught by one of the wide receivers. The most unlikely option was for the tight end, who is in the middle of the chaos, to actually out-jump the crowd of defenders and catch the ball. That was simply too improbable under the circumstances. Regardless, Clay Brown counters, "I wasn't playing for a tipped ball!"

Following the snap of the football, McMahon dropped back beyond the fifty yard line. The BYU linemen and Phillips held out the SMU rush for three seconds, and McMahon launched a spiral high into the cold, foggy San Diego night air. Even though SMU only rushed three lineman, one of the ends, Richard Neeley, nearly got to McMahon. It is a good thing Phillips heard that he was supposed to stay home and block because he had to make a critical clean-up block on the SMU defensive end. If Phillips hadn't been there, McMahon would not have had time to get the pass away. The other running back, Eric Lane, made no pretense of staying home during the play. He sprinted out of the backfield as soon as the ball was snapped. Phillips later asked Lane what he was doing, and he replied, "I wasn't going to miss out on all of that excitement in the end zone, and I was going to be there for the tipped ball!"[16] It was another lucky break that the main SMU rush at McMahon came on the left side of the BYU line—where Phillips was set up to block. If the rush had come on the other side there would have been no blocking help from the backfield.

As the ball descended into the end zone, SMU's NFL-bound defensive back Wes Hopkins leaped high above the turf and got one of his hands on the ball at the apex of his jump, just as Clay Brown hit his apex and wrapped his arms around it too. SMU defensive back Dick Blaylock was right there too, fighting Brown for the ball. By the time they hit the turf at the back of the end zone, Brown had the ball firmly in his grasp. The refs signaled a BYU touchdown. Unbelievable pandemonium erupted in the stadium. Tony Roberts, the radio announcer for the game was literally screaming into the microphone as he explained, "Back to throw. Last down. No time on the clock. It's up in the air. It is deep. It is . . . ? He caught it! It's a touchdown! Touchdown on the last play, and Brigham Young has won it. A miracle catch!"[17]

Blaylock said that he saw the ball all the way in and jumped up to bat it away. "That is all we needed to do, bat it down." He said he has no idea what happened or how the ball got through his hands. "It doesn't seem possible. It doesn't even seem real." Blaylock's comment summarizes what everyone who saw the play thought too. There is just no way that ball should have made it through the mass of hands and arms swinging at it to land in Clay Brown's hands. SMU head coach Ron Meyer was quoted as saying, "I never thought he'd come down with the ball like that. How did that guy catch that thing? We had everybody in the world there. It was incredible."[18] SMU running back Craig James was quoted as saying that if he had had a gun with him, he would have shot McMahon's pass out of the night sky. Then, he allowed, "Given the way things were going for us at that point, I probably would have missed."

The fight for the football between Brown and the Mustang defensive backs continued on the ground, but Brown had clear possession of the football. Both McMahon and Edwards reported that their first reaction was to look around for a penalty flag—not that they thought something was wrong with the play; it was just so surreal that they feared the play would be called back. No penalties. No flags. And the score was tied: SMU 45, BYU 45. Bedlam ensued.

Hopkins complained that he caught the ball. Replays and photographs of the play prove him half right: he has his arms around the ball, all right, but Brown's arms are inside of Hopkins' arms and around the pigskin when they hit the turf in the end zone. It is clearly a BYU touchdown. Even if it was a tie, which it was not, it would have been a BYU touchdown. In that situation a tie goes to the offense.

Brown's response to the claim that Hopkins caught the ball is pretty straightforward: "Why did he claim he caught the ball? That doesn't make any sense. In that situation, the only thing for a defensive back to do is to knock the ball down. It would make no sense to try for an interception in that situation: No time on the clock, the play is in the end zone. You *knock* the ball *away*."[19] That, of course, is just what SMU's all-American John Simmons had done with McMahon's bomb to Braga at the end of the first half. Just like at the end of the game, an interception on that play wouldn't have made any difference in the game, so Simmons batted the ball away.

Brown also said that hanging on to the ball after they were all on the ground was the most work he had done all night. "I had three guys on top of me, trying to take the ball. They were tugging and tugging and tugging."[20]

My hometown newspaper interviewed me about the game when I was home for the holidays. When asked about Brown's catch, I explained that we played a lot of pick-up basketball at BYU, before and after football practice. I had also been on an intramural basketball team with Clay, and he was a very tough and tenacious rebounder. That is how I viewed his catch of the Hail Mary in the Holiday Bowl. Clay simply went up for the rebound, threw some elbows, and came down with the ball. We had all seen him do that many times before on the Smith Fieldhouse basketball courts.

Interestingly Jim McMahon was also an awesome basketball player—all-State at Roy High School. He was a great point guard and knew how to get the ball to the right people at the right time, just as he did on the final play in the bowl game. Using their all-around athletic ability, Jim and Clay meshed perfectly to pull off the greatest no-time-on-the-clock Hail Mary play in a bowl game—ever. Finally, they had orchestrated a realization of the dream that Clay's wife had had the year before.

After Brown's miracle catch, Kurt Gunther trotted onto the field for the extra point: the point that would also provide the margin of victory for BYU, secure the football program its first bowl victory, and provide vindication for the BYU pass-happy offensive scheme and its visionary

Clay Brown (85)

coach, LaVell Edwards. That extra point kick would provide a measure of redemption for the last-second loss from the year before—on a missed kick.

Just like Brent Johnson in 1979, Kurt Gunther had not been called on to win any games for BYU during the 1980 season. Other than the opening day loss to New Mexico, BYU had blown out all of its opponents. The Cougars scored 83 points against UTEP, 70 against Utah State, 56 against Utah, 54 against UNLV, 52 against Wyoming, and so on. Gunther had been a dependable kicker for BYU all year but had not kicked a pressure kick anything like he faced in the final play of Holiday Bowl III. BYU had attempted several two-point conversions during the game, trying to close the gap on the Mustangs. This meant Gunther had kicked only one extra point in the game. Indeed as Ray Scott opined, "all" of the pressure was now on the special team: Gunther's team. "Kurt Gunther will try to win it for BYU."[21]

GAME LESSON # 8
WHEN THE GAME IS ON THE LINE, KEEP YOUR EYE ON THE BALL AND FOLLOW THROUGH!

Many of us wonder how well we will perform when the game is on the line, so to speak, when everything hinges on our ability to block out the stress and the noise and do our job. Whether in work, sports, school, church, family, or whatever, we all have those questions. McMahon, Brown, Schoepflin, Phillips, Braga, Davis, Whittingham, Redd, Titensor, Holmoe, Sikahema, Johnson, the offensive line, and many others had come through just when it was needed. Now it was Kurt Gunther's turn—his turn to perform a task considered all but automatic by everyone except the one who had to do it. As he fastened his helmet and headed into the mist, he knew full well that nothing is ever automatic on a football field, and there was plenty to worry about—especially given what had happened to the BYU football team the year before.

I was not overly worried about the kick because I had seen Gunther make some pressure-filled kicks on the JV team the year before and he was unfazed by those situations. Of course, those JV games were not the same as a post-season varsity bowl game, but as anyone knows who has competed at any level in sports, music, or whatever, the pressure of the moment is nearly the same no matter what level you are playing on. A high school basketball player at the foul line with the game tied and two seconds left feels the same kind of pressure as a collegiate player at the foul line in a close game in the NCAA tournament.

In fact, Gunther had won more than one game for the JV team in 1979, including a game-ending kick that gave us a victory over Snow College 42 to 41. In that game, not unlike Holiday Bowl III, we were losing 35 to 7 in the first quarter and then, behind a five-touchdown effort from our tailback, Jimmy Jones, we came back to tie the game with only a few minutes remaining. Gunther made the extra point, and we won by one point. As we ran off the field after the extra point, several players slapped me on the back and yelled congratulations to me as the holder for the kick.

I was not sure what the fuss was about, since I thought it was a fairly routine extra point kick. When I asked what they were talking about, they told me that the snap had been high and behind me so I had to turn and catch the snap and then turn back around and get the ball down in time for Gunther to make the kick. I was focused on getting the hold right, so I did not realize that the snap had been high and wide. The extra split second it took me to get the ball down and ready to kick threw off Gunther's timing to some degree so he had to adjust his approach. None of that bothered him, and he nailed the kick to win the game.

The same focus and attitude were about to serve Gunther well as he ran on the field to attempt the most important, pressure-filled kick in BYU history. He knew he had to keep his eye on the ball. He absolutely could not look up. He had to get his steps right, complete his kick, and follow through. He had to stick to his regular, smooth routine—there could be no interruptions, no glitches. Yet, all of that was crowded by the memory of the final kick in the 1979 Holiday Bowl.

It was not a given that Gunther was going to be the kicker for the 1980 BYU team at all. Another kicker was slated as the starter prior to the season, but that kicker was ruled ineligible and dropped from the roster just before the first game. Gunther had been pulled out of a BYU classroom and told he was making the trip to New Mexico as the kicker for the team just three hours before he needed to leave. He had to get packed and get his mind around the fact that he had just been called up to be the varsity kicker. In the confusion of that moment, Kurt forgot to pack his helmet. Some BYU fans who were travelling to the New Mexico game on a private plane took the helmet down with them. Kurt's concentration on the field was much better.[22]

In an article by Bob Hudson in the *Provo Daily Herald* following the first-game loss to New Mexico, Gunther said: "If I had a pressure field goal, I would try to block out what the actual situation is." Although that is a sound strategy, the circumstances surrounding the final kick in the 1980 Holiday Bowl would make that approach nearly impossible. Gunther would later explain, "I remembered the team missing a win last year because of a kick, and I wanted to make sure it didn't happen again."[23]

As if the kick and the circumstances around it in the bowl game were not stressful enough, just before he ran on to the field for the final kick, Gunther heard Coach Scovil tell Coach Edwards that the team should go for a two-point conversion, rather than risk another botched kick like in the 1979 game. That was probably a legitimate idea for Coach Scovil, but fortunately Coach Edwards opted to go for the seemingly more automatic kick to seal the victory.

Had Coach Edwards known the mini-drama that was about to unfold with that extra-point kick, he might have given the nod to Coach Scovil's request. As it was, Gunther ran on to the field with Coach Scovil's demand ringing in his ears, which caused him to focus even more on the final kick in Holiday Bowl II. Luckily Gunther heard both Coach Edwards and McMahon agree "Let's kick it." That helped Kurt muster the confidence to weather the complications that would soon confront him. Regardless, given those developments, it is little wonder that Gunther had Brent Johnson on his mind as he lined up for the final, decisive extra-point kick.

GAME LESSON #9

WHEN OPPOSITION IS IN YOUR FACE,

TAKE A DEEP BREATH AND LET IT FLY

The extra-point formation was called, and the team lined up on the ball as the holder, Schoepflin, prepared to call the signals. Corey Pace, the long-snapper for BYU, settled over the football as he had done hundreds of times before in games and in practice and waited for the signal from Schoepflin. Extra point attempts are rarely missed. The routine for the long-snapper, the holder and the kicker become so polished that it seems almost a "gimme" to those watching the action. However the orchestration between the snapper, holder, and kicker is so precise that many things can, and do, go wrong, especially in game-on-the-line situations. The pressure can be intense, and even a little moisture or dirt on the ball or a drop of sweat in the holder's eye can result in a miss.

Out of the three people involved directly in the extra-point transaction, the snapper, the holder, and the kicker, the snapper may have the most difficult or at least the most contorted and convoluted job of the bunch. He has to hike the ball between his legs, while he is bent over and looking back through his legs, dressed in bulky football pads and a helmet, knowing full well that as soon as he snaps the ball a 250-plus pound opponent is lined up about eight inches from him with instructions to try to knock him senseless. From that contorted position, he has to deliver a perfect, rifle-shot spiral between his legs to a spot right in front of the holder, seven or eight yards behind him, that is much smaller than the strike zone in baseball. In this case, 230-pound Corey Pace lined up for the snap with SMU's 265-pound nose guard, future NFL star Michael Carter, positioned right in Corey's face.

Before the bowl game, the *Salt Lake Tribune* reported that Gary Zauner, the special teams coach for BYU, argued that the center is the main man on the special teams. "Everything begins with a good snap of the ball."[24] It is also interesting that in that article, which was entitled "Call 'Em Nuts or Special," Coach Zauner was quoted as saying that he had watched a lot of film of SMU and had something special in mind for the game, without giving any further details. The article concludes with the thought that one big play from the special team "crazies" during the game might be the difference in the outcome.[25] The "something special," it turns out, was the onside kick, which worked perfectly when it was really needed. As it turned out, several big plays from the special teams were needed, along with many other big plays on both offense and defense, to orchestrate the comeback and victory.

In reality an extra-point kick is still nearly a twenty-yard kick, once you factor in the end zone and the distance between the line of scrimmage and the holder. Super Bowl games have been lost on kicking glitches, and every year important college and pro games are lost by misses on what, on the surface, appear to be routine kicks from close range. When Schoepflin raised his left hand from the position of the spot, which was the signal for the ball to be snapped, for a moment nothing happened. Gunther leaned forward, leaned some more, and . . . nothing. The ball did not come. Gunther took a small stutter step because the ball was supposed to be in Schoepflin's hands by then but it was not there. The stutter step was necessary to keep Gunther from losing his balance because of the delay with the snap. He did neither.

Schoepflin also recalls the delayed snap. He says that he too was thinking about the missed kick from the year before because he was the holder for Brent Johnson during the 1979 season. He recalled that the main thing running through his mind on that final kick in the 1980 game was simply, "We really have to make this point."[26] He remembered there was the briefest moment of panic when the ball did not come as ordered. "It didn't come cleanly for sure, but just as I began to wonder what to do next, the ball came and I got it down for the kick," he explained. It was fortunate that Schoepflin had enough focus to catch the snap just as he was starting to wonder if or when the ball was going to come. It would have been easy to lose focus and panic in that situation. The loss of concentration caused by the delay followed by the surprise delivery could have caused him to bobble or fumble the snap

Other complications added to the drama of Gunther's kick. In 1980 placekickers routinely used a small one- to two-inch high kicking block or tee to elevate the ball off the turf and provide more room for the kicker's toe to get under the tip of the ball and launch it into the air. Because of the delayed snap, and knowing that Gunther was already on approach, so to speak, Schoepflin knew he needed to hurry and get the ball down on the kicking tee or it might be too late for Gunther. In that rush, he barely got the ball on the tee and most of the tip of the ball was hanging off of the edge of the tee. Kurt says he had a brief thought that the ball might slip off of the tee just as he got to it. The end zone replay of the kick shows the tenuous ball placement on the tee and provides a good view of what Gunther was looking at as he approached the ball.

There was one other thing that bothered Gunther as he approached the ball. At the time, holders were taught that for extra-point kicks there was no need to adjust the laces of the football to have them facing the goal post once the snap was received. The thinking was that an extra point kick is so close there is really no need to adjust the laces to help the kicker get more power into the football, as is necessary with longer field goals. For longer field goals, holders were taught to spin the ball on the tee to make sure the laces are lined up facing the goal post. This would theoretically help the kicker on the longer kicks because his foot would be hitting the solid leather of the ball, rather than the more unstable and uneven laces, and he would feel safer in really hammering the ball if his foot was going to hit full leather, rather than the laces or half ball and half laces. And for the longer kicks, it was important for the laces to be spinning along the line of the flight of the ball so they would not cause any air interference to push the ball off course. For the shorter kicks, the air interference was thought to be a non-issue. We spent many hours practicing catching the snap and placing the ball on the tee while spinning the laces to the correct spot for the longer kicks.

Because the holders were taught to not worry about the laces on extra-point kicks, the kicker and holder were at the mercy of chance as to where the laces would end up after the snap. Sometimes the laces would be facing the kicker, sometimes facing the goal, and sometimes at other points of the compass around the ball. Most of the time on an extra-point kick, kickers were not overly concerned where the laces lined up. However on Gunther's final kick in the bowl game, in addition to the drama of the comeback and the Hail Mary play, the pressure of knowing that some coaches thought it would be better to go for two points rather than risk another botched kick, the delayed snap, the miss from the year before, and the precarious ball placement on the tee, when Kurt looked down at the ball when he was on the approach, there were the laces facing directly back at him. Kurt said that on top of everything else, that, too, seemed like a bad omen.[27]

The miraculous BYU comeback was in jeopardy of a botched extra-point kick—exactly what Coach Scovil was worried about. In 1980, if a game was tied at the end of regulation play, there would be no overtime or sudden death. The game simply ended in a tie. BYU would have still been winless in bowl games, and Holiday Bowl III would have faded into obscurity, much like Holiday Bowl II. It would have been an incredible comeback that fell just short of victory. Coach Edwards would have been haunted by another missed kick to end an exciting bowl game that BYU could have won.

Gunther's stutter step can be seen if you watch the film closely—especially the replay from the end zone camera. For a split second his timing and routine are off as he leans forward, expecting the ball to be there. That split second was an eternity for Gunther. It looks as though he almost loses his balance before he strides back into the kick. Often, when athletes find themselves in clutch situations to end a game with either victory or defeat seemingly in their hands, or at some other critical moment in their competition, they will say that everything appeared to play out in slow motion. Here, for Gunther, it was no psychological anomaly—it really did play out in slow motion.

But, no sooner had he stutter-stepped than the ball was delivered safely to Schoepflin's hands and Schoepflin placed it down for the kick. A split second later, Gunther's foot struck the ball—or the laces, to be more precise. There was no doubt about the outcome of the kick—even if it was a little out of rhythm. Schoepflin says that all of the drama evaporated as soon as Kurt's foot hit the ball because he immediately knew the kick was good.

BYU 46 SMU 45.

Later, Gunther asked Corey Pace what had happened with the snap and the delay. Pace said there was so much excitement generated by the Hail Mary play, he had to take a moment to gather himself before he snapped the ball—to make sure he could get the snap where it needed to be. He took a breath to calm down and then let it fly. Pace also explains that, for some reason, the game official took extra time in placing the ball down for the extra-point attempt so Pace could settle in over the ball. That delay also added to the slow-motion feel of the last play and heightened the pressure of the moment, especially for Pace.

It is another small miracle that Pace was able to deliver a near-perfect snap after that brief hitch. Many people would have wilted under the pressure of that moment. Earlier in the game there had been a botched snap (by another center) on a punt that resulted in a safety for SMU and, after Sikahema's punt return touchdown in the second quarter, a fake extra-point attempt had failed. On that play, Schoepflin had had to scramble around behind the line of scrimmage as Gunther had tried to block for him. The play ended up with an incomplete pass in the end zone. Those two plays also weighed on the minds of the extra point team as they lined up to win the game.

As if Pace did not already have enough to worry about in snapping the ball for the extra point, he was scheduled to get married the next morning in the Los Angeles LDS Temple. Mormons are not known for bachelor parties, but Holiday Bowl III may be the most memorable bachelor party in history. People are still talking and writing about it over thirty years later.

No one in the stands, the parking lot, or watching at home knew how close that final extra point was to disaster at several levels. It is inconceivable now to think about BYU botching a second consecutive Holiday Bowl game on a failed kick from close range at the end of the game. Thankfully Pace, Schoepflin, Gunther and the rest of that special team were able to step up and complete the play.

Some may not even realize that Clay Brown also lined up to block on that extra-point attempt. He said he simply concentrated on his blocking assignment and made sure he plugged up a hole. One of the iconic pictures of the end of the game is an end zone shot taken during the extra point kick. That is a favorite picture because it shows the scoreboard with the time at ":00" and the score tied at 45 to 45. People can be seen standing across the top of the far end zone stands. Those are some of the people who were lucky enough to make it back into the stadium (or who stopped their exodus in time) once the BYU comeback became a reality. The picture is also exciting because it shows that Brown did more than just plug a hole. An SMU player was launched airborne by Clay's block. A poster-size print of that photo hangs prominently in the Holiday Bowl offices at Qualcomm Stadium in San Diego.

None of the drama with the extra point takes away from the many spectacular plays that led up to the moment of the game-winning kick, particularly the last-second bomb from McMahon to Brown—which will go down in college football history as one of the greatest desperation pass completions ever. If miracles happen in sports, surely that Hail Mary pass was one of them.

Ray Scott captured the color of it all as he wrapped up the broadcast. As credits rolled on the screen he said:

"We're going to watch it one more time. This is the touchdown that tied the game. This is Jim McMahon, the NCAA spectacular passing leader of the season firing that ball almost sixty yards in the air. Number 85 Clay Brown in that mass of players came up with the football because he just seemed to want it. Here is the point that won the game by Kurt Gunther, off of a hold by Bill Schoepflin. . . . I don't know how you could ever top this one."[28]

The entire 1980 BYU football team and its fans were beneficiaries of the hard lessons the team had learned the year before. Gunther was also a grateful beneficiary of the lessons Brent Johnson taught him about the ending of Holiday Bowl II. Kurt considers Brent to be his mentor. If Gunther had not been so focused on keeping his eye on the ball, the

Opposite top, from left: Chuck Ehin (78), Corey Pace (55)
Opposite bottom, from left: Charles Bruton (27), Wes Hopkins (46), Mitch Willis (98), Bill Schoepflin (43), Ryan Tibbitts (18)

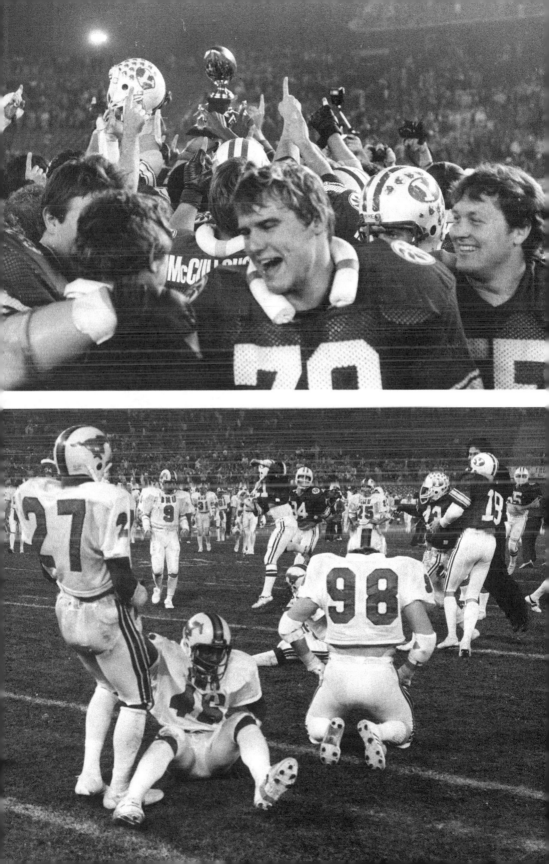

memory of what had happened at the conclusion of Holiday Bowl II in 1979, coupled with the delayed snap and the other problems, could have caused him to panic, lose his rhythm and focus, and miss the kick. Fortunately Gunther was ready for those contingencies and kept his cool. And on a foggy night in San Diego, as the ball arched into the mist and through the uprights and the scoreboard flicked to BYU 46 SMU 45, a legacy for the ages was born.

AS IF THE GAME WASN'T THRILLING ENOUGH

Our itinerary indicated that after the game we were to be boarded on our charter flight by 10:45—no later, due to a noise curfew at Lindbergh Field that limited late-night takeoffs —and arrive in Salt Lake City by one o'clock in the morning and then arrive back at the Smith Fieldhouse in Provo an hour and fifteen minutes later. None of that would go like clockwork—but then, neither did anything else that night.

Due to the noise curfew, if the BYU flight did not take off by 10:45 p.m., it was not going to leave that night. As a result, after the game, team management kept pleading with the BYU coaches, players, and travel party to hustle up and get to the airport. That was not an easy assignment given the unbelievable ending that had just occurred. Everyone wanted to celebrate, not shower and pack up for the trip home. Finally the travel coordinators and athletic directors somehow got those of us who were returning to Utah onto the buses and headed to the airport.

As it turned out, the Salt Lake Airport was socked in with a winter inversion, and the flight was unable to land on time in SLC. A couple of attempts to punch the airplane down through the fog failed. A team of specialists from the airport was called in to seed the clouds in order to create an opening for the aircraft. After circling Salt Lake for nearly an hour, the pilots made one final attempt to land before they would have needed to divert to the Boise, Idaho, airport because the airplane was running low on fuel. The pilots nosed the airplane down through the thick soup and, at the last possible moment, saw a runway light and were able to make the landing in Salt Lake. Apparently it was a night for success at the last possible moment.

Because of the late landing in SLC, the buses that were supposed to transport us home to Provo from the airport had been told that we had diverted to Boise so they had left. We had to wait at the SLC airport for another 45 minutes for the buses to return and finally arrived back in Provo at about 4:00 a.m. I don't recall anyone being particularly tired—even at that hour. Provo was still alive and buzzing about the game, at least the people who hadn't turned off their television sets, locked their doors, and gone to bed before it was over.

I Don't Know
How You Could
Top This One

The 1980 Miracle Bowl is consistently listed as one of the top ten finishes in college football history. After the telecast, Ray Scott knew he had just witnessed a contest destined to go down in football lore. (Ray had been the voice of the Green Bay Packers during the Vince Lombardi era and had called the famed "Ice Bowl" in December 1967 between the Dallas Cowboys and Green Bay Packers and who had also announced four Super Bowls and seven NFL championship games.) This is how he summed it up: "Brigham Young in an absolutely unpredictable, wild finish has defeated SMU in one of the most spectacular college football endings I have ever . . . ever seen. . . . This is one of the most improbable, fantastic finishes we have ever seen."[1] Radio announcer Tony Roberts exclaimed, "I don't believe it! I don't believe it, and yet I saw it!"[2] That was a near universal reaction to the wild ending to the game.

Just a few days before the Holiday Bowl, on December 14, 1980, Scott had called the action for the NFL playoff game between the Minnesota Vikings and Cleveland Brown, which ended on a famous Hail Mary pass from Viking quarterback Tommy Kramer to receiver Ahmad Rashad to beat the Browns and advance in the playoffs. At the end of the Holiday Bowl broadcast, Scott mentioned that NFL playoff game and exclaimed, "We've done it again!" Then he concluded that the BYU comeback and ending were even more dramatic, "I don't know how you could ever top this one!"[3]

In its 1996 post-season college bowl game issue, *TV Guide* listed the "Best Bowls of All Time."[4] The 1980 Holiday Bowl was listed as number five. In 2002 ESPN.com included "McMahon's Prayer"[5] on its list of College Football's Fantastic Finishes. In 2003 ESPN's "Page 2" listed Holiday Bowl III as the number four greatest bowl game of all time.[6] In 2006 CBSTV uploaded highlights from the game on YouTube and labeled the segment "Greatest Bowl Comeback Ever?"[7] By 2014 that YouTube segment had over a half-million views and people were still adding laudatory comments to the segment on a regular basis.

The 1980 Holiday Bowl is an ESPN "Classic" football game and is included in EA Sports' NCAA College Football 2005 computer game as one of the "College Classics" games where players can try to recreate the conclusion of the game or create some other ending to the game. That segment of the game is described as "America's Most Exciting Bowl Game." Players pick up the game when the score is 45 to 31 and try to finish out with a win on their computer game consoles. This is how it is explained:

> 1980 BYU vs. SMU
>
> The Situation: "America's Most Exciting Bowl Game," otherwise known as the Holiday Bowl, was an old-fashioned shootout in the 1980 version of the game between BYU and SMU. BYU is trailing 45-31 late in the 4th quarter. Can you lead a "Cougar Comeback," just as the legendary BYU quarterback did over 20 years ago?
>
> The Strategy: This is one of the toughest of all the College Classics. You begin by kicking an extra point. Go ahead and blast it through to bring the score to 45–26. Afterwards, you'll have to execute an onside kick. The best way to do this is to point the kick directly at the ground, at a 45 degree angle to the opposition's line. Go halfway up on the left side of the kick meter and stop in the yellow. This gives you the best chance at [sic] recover the kick, probably off of a deflection. You can also try to aim a kick waist-high directly at a player, and try to bounce it off of him, then recover that.
>
> Even if you don't get the onside kick, you can still pull off the win. You'll just have to stop them on subsequent plays, calling timeouts in between. You need three total scores, and that means two onside kicks need to go your way, or you have to pick up a turnover on defense, or you have to wait out an extra opposition drive and strike quickly when you get the ball. On defense, you know they'll run to burn clock, so stack against it. On offense, use five wide receiver sets to spread the field and get the most players open as possible.

In 2007, following the dramatic "Statue of Liberty" victory by Boise State over Oklahoma in the Fiesta Bowl, msn.foxsports.com asked the question, "Where does the 2007 Fiesta Bowl rank?" In that article, Pete Fiutak wrote: "For the improbable and impossible, the 2007 Fiesta Bowl still can't quite touch the 1980 Holiday Bowl, when BYU was down 45 to 25 to SMU with less than four minutes to play, and got a blocked punt, a defensive stand, and a Hail Mary, or as BYU called it, a "Save the Game" pass from Jim McMahon to win 46–45."[8]

In January 2011 deepintosports.com posted a story entitled "10 Most Dramatic Bowl Games of All Time—NCAA College Football."[9] It ranked the 1980 Holiday Bowl as number eight. In February 2011, sportsthenandnow.com ran a story entitled "Do You Believe in Miracles? Top 20 'Miracles' in Sports History." The 1980 Holiday Bowl is listed as number 11. Not surprisingly the February 1980 "Miracle on Ice," when Team USA Hockey beat the Soviet Union to advance to the gold medal game in the Lake Placid Winter Olympics, is ranked number 1. Number 10 on the list is the 1954 Milan Miracle, when tiny Milan High School won the Indiana state basketball championship with a last-second shot. This game was the inspiration for the wonderful 1986 movie "Hoosiers."[10]

In the fall of 2011, the website Yardbarker listed the Miracle Bowl as the number three college Hail Mary play of all time. (The 1984 "Hail Flutie" and 1994 "Miracle at Michigan" were chosen as numbers one and two, respectively.) In December 2011 Bleacherreport.com senior writer Dan Vasta compiled a list of the "50 Most Exciting College Football Bowl Games of All Time." In that compilation he lists the Miracle Bowl as 47 out of 50, with number 50 (somewhat confusingly) being the most exciting. Vasta notes that McMahon threw for 446 yards and 4 TDs and concludes: "Well, the miracle was answered as McMahon connected on a third attempted pass to Clay Brown as he was surrounded by four different Mustang defenders. They tacked on the extra point and pulled off the comeback, 46–45, in arguably the most dramatic finish to any bowl game in the history of the sport."[11]

The Miracle Bowl is sandwiched between the 1979 Cotton Bowl where Notre Dame defeated Houston in the famous Joe Montana "Chicken Soup Bowl" and the January 1984 Miami Nebraska Orange Bowl where Nebraska went for a two-point conversion rather than kicking an extra point to tie, failed in the attempt, and lost the game. The greatest bowl victory, in Vasta's opinion, was the 2006 national title Rose Bowl between USC and Texas where Vince Young led Texas to victory over the Matt Leinart and Reggie Bush–led Trojans 41 to 38.

In April 2013 top10onlinecolleges.org ran an article entitled "10 Iconic Moments in College Football History." The Miracle Bowl came in at number 5—just behind the 1967 USC/UCLA classic and just before the 1969 Texas/Arkansas "Game of the Century." In that article Schoepflin's punt block is called the "miracle block." The 1982 California/Stanford "The Play" game is the number one iconic moment—thanks to the Stanford band.

In August 2013 BYUtv aired a program entitled "BYU Football: Top 50 Plays." In that program Vai Sikahema's 83-yard punt return was listed as play number 39, Bill Schoepflin's punt block was listed at number 23 and the McMahon-to-Brown Hail Mary play was listed as number 2. As indicated in the broadcast, there is room for debate about the order of these plays, and the top ten plays were chosen by fans rather than football specialists or professionals.[12]

Many, including me, think the McMahon-to-Brown pass should have been ranked number 1, given the national attention that game and play still generate and what it did for the BYU football program, but that is how the votes came out. As it is, the number 1 play, as chosen by the fans, is the 2006 John Beck to Jonny Harline no-time-on-the-clock game winner against Utah in Salt Lake City. Number 3 is the 1990 Ty Detmer scramble and touchdown to Mike Salido in the third quarter of the game against number-one-ranked Miami. The top ten plays are all amazing plays, for sure, but none have come close to generating the type of national attention—for more than thirty years—as the McMahon-to-Brown Hail Mary.

As recently as September 2014, Matt Brown, for sportsonearth.com, listed the McMahon-to-Brown Hail Mary number four of the "Best College Football Hail Marys" of all time.[13]

Bruce Binkowski has been with the Holiday Bowl since its inception in 1978. He is currently the executive director. Bruce also is the Qualcomm Stadium PA announcer. Bruce explains, "I have called many exciting Charger and Padres games and many other sporting events, including pro playoff games, major league baseball all-star games, and even a Super Bowl. When people ask me which sporting event is the most memorable to me, I still go back to the 1980 Holiday Bowl. Nothing has ever topped it."[14]

So in every decade since the game, the 1980 Holiday Bowl has ranked with the greatest finishes in college football bowl history. The game is still being recognized and discussed in the press and earning accolades for the superstars of the game. Replays of the game can still be seen on sports channels running the greatest games ever played, and sometimes at the most unexpected times. On Thanksgiving Day 2011, my children flipped on the television while we were visiting their grandmother in Idaho and, believe it or not, KBYU was replaying the complete 1980 Holiday Bowl—on Thanksgiving morning no less—that many years later!

THE DAYS AND WEEKS AFTER

McMahon, Brown, and Coach Edwards became overnight stars as a result of the game. All three stayed in San Diego after the game to deal with interviews and other public relations matters, and were in heavy demand around the country for several days. Jim McMahon, Craig James, and Michael Carter were named as the official MVPs of the game—although at the end of Mizlou broadcast, Glen Titensor of BYU is identified as the defensive MVP. The radio broadcasters identified SMU's Craig James and Michael Carter as the MVPs.

McMahon still holds the Holiday Bowl record for touchdown passes with four. Brown holds the record for touchdown receptions with three. BYU seniors Glen Titensor, Glen Redd, and Nick Eyre were invited to play in the East-West Shrine game. Clay Brown was invited to play in the Hula Bowl. Brown and Eyre were invited to play in the Senior Bowl. The Holiday Bowl game was replayed almost constantly at "The Star Palace" dance club in Provo and at numerous other restaurants and other establishments around Provo. Thank heaven for VHS tape.

A few days after the game, a button started circulating among Cougar fans that read: "I Stayed. 46/45." One trial lawyer I know, a BYU graduate, told me that he and his law partner used to listen to the last four minutes of the game to get themselves pumped up for courtroom battles. Another group of businessmen fans developed and marketed a soft drink called "The Catch" to commemorate the game and the McMahon-to-Brown Hail Mary. It was not on the market long, so it probably did not sell very well anywhere but Provo, but BYU students raised many cans of the drink to celebrate the victory. The iconic photo of Brown's Hail Mary catch adorned the can of soda.

On January 28, 1981, the university hosted an event in the Marriott Center to honor the team. Over 10,000 fans attended the event. Team members were given various memorabilia, including an early version of a "boom box" radio and cassette player, along with a cassette tape of the last four minutes of the game from the Mutual Radio broadcast featuring Tony Roberts. Each boom box was adorned with a gold plaque, which included an inscription of the player's name along with "1980 Holiday Bowl." The players were each introduced to the audience and admitted to "The Four Minute Miracle Club" by the Provo Chamber of Commerce. WAC commissioner Joe Kearney attended the event and presented the team with the WAC Championship trophy. Vinnie Vinson represented the Holiday Bowl and presented the bowl trophy. He also thanked the team for making the Holiday Bowl the most talked-about bowl game in the country in its first three years. Our WAC championship rings for the 1980 season prominently feature the Holiday Bowl victory and score, as well as the WAC championship. And there are three smaller blue glass jewels placed on one side to commemorate the third Holiday Bowl—the first bowl victory for the team.

The mayors of Provo and San Diego, Jim Ferguson and Pete Wilson, respectively, thanked the team for putting both cities on the map. LDS General Authority Paul Dunn spoke and reminded the team of Winston Churchill's famous statement about never giving up, which certainly applied to the Cougars in Holiday Bowl III. President Jeffrey R. Holland also spoke and advised that the team's "never-say-die" example had inspired the whole country. Glen Redd and Coach Edwards spoke for the team, and highlights of the game were viewed as the audience cheered and Athletic Director Glen Tuckett provided narration.

Not everyone in Provo was caught up in the euphoria. Certain artifacts of the game, such as McMahon's and Brown's game jerseys, Kurt Gunter's shoe, and the Holiday Bowl trophy were placed on display in the library for several weeks. Apparently the display and the fawning of BYU fans irritated a cartoonist for the *Daily Universe* who drew a cartoon of the display but added a few other items: Calvin Close's toothbrush, Vai Sikahema's sock, Nick Eyre's band aid, Kurt Gunther's foot powder, a bottle of Miracle Whip and so forth. The cartoon also depicts fans crowded around the display with a study desk in the background covered with cobwebs.

Gradually, life settled back to normal. The seniors graduated or otherwise moved on, and the underclassmen prepared for spring football as a warm up to the 1981 season. The game itself would live on in such places as ESPN Classics, KBYU Friday Night Fandemonium, BYUtv, and other such outlets. The iconic photo of Brown's Hail Mary catch was chosen for the cover of the 25th Anniversary Holiday Bowl Program for the 2002 game between Kansas State and Arizona State. Recollections from McMahon, Brown, and Dickerson are highlighted in the "25 Years of Thrills" section of the program. The Holiday Bowl retains a sizeable collection of programs and other memorabilia from the bowl games, going back to the beginning. They have many programs left over for most of the games. But all of the programs for the 1980 game are long gone. I'm pleased that I still have mine.

CONCLUSION

The unbelievable ending to the Miracle Bowl still inspires football fans, particularly BYU fans, all over the country. Almost daily somebody watches "The Greatest Bowl Comeback Ever?" segment on YouTube.[1] Something about that improbable comeback is timeless in its appeal to fans around the world. The gut-wrenching drama of the game is undeniable.

Contrary to the joke I and others have been telling for thirty-plus years, and will continue to tell about Catholics, Mormons, Baptists, and many other religions teaming up to beat the powerful and daunting—and allegedly well-paid—1980 Mustangs of SMU, who probably had some Methodists on their team, it wasn't really a battle of religions that night. It was an unbelievable, exciting comeback in a memorable, even miraculous, football game engineered by an amazing quarterback and his team, all fighting for a visionary coach who was well past his due to win a bowl game.

No one can say for certain what would have happened to the BYU football program if the team had been embarrassed that night in San Diego. The team would have been zero for five in bowl games. Instead of the confidence and swagger that game gave the program, the team and coach would have entered the 1981 season at least somewhat humiliated and demoralized. Coach Edwards hints at what the program would have been looking at when he says that it cannot be overemphasized how important that game was to the program, both for the fact of a victory in a bowl game and the spectacular way it came about. BYU football was on its way to a national championship. Both Robbie Bosco and Vai Sika-hema, stars on the national championship team in 1984, do not hesitate to state that without the 1980 Miracle Bowl, which also influenced the Holiday Bowl victories in 1981 and 1983 over opponents in a power conference, there would likely be no national championship in 1984.

In a real way, the 1980 Holiday Bowl Hail Mary was not just a single play for that game. It was a Hail Mary for the whole BYU football program. It was a Hail Mary to overcome the four prior bowl losses and to prove that BYU could win the big one. And that is exactly what it did.

Sportswriter and football analyst Michael Silver, writing for *Sports Illustrated* in an article entitled "American Beauty," made the following observation:

"Here's the deal with football players: To be a good one, you've got to force your body to perform actions that your mind is dead-set against. For a player to accept that bargain on a consistent basis, he'd better have a sense of something greater than individual gain, be it faith in a god or a coach, a bond with his teammates or a profound fear of failure. Football filters out insincerity in a hurry."

On December 19, 1980, all of those factors came into play for the BYU football team. The "insincerity" of the first half gave way to "something greater" in the second half—with spectacular results.

For those of us on the field and the sidelines that San Diego December night, the 1980 Holiday Bowl—The Miracle Bowl—will always be an amazing, crazy memory. McMahon's last pass will hang in the cool, foggy air forever, and Gunther's final kick will be straight and true—if a bit late. The game has inspired the members of that team from that day to the present. It taught us about teamwork. It taught us to trust one another, and it taught us not to quit. Since December 1980, I have personally used the lessons taught by that game in every aspect of my life.

The game will always stand for things that the team taught us that night—what Mel Farr taught us: never say "impossible"; what Vai Sika-hema taught us: when things look hopeless, take a risk and run like you have nothing to lose; what Bill Schoepflin taught us: test the opposition's vulnerabilities, and then exploit them; what Jim McMahon taught us: never, never, never give up; what Matt Braga taught us: sometimes success comes if you dive at a problem and hang on until the dust clears; what Lee Johnson taught us: learn to trust yourself; what Clay Brown taught us: just want it more than those trying to stop you; what Corey Pace taught us: when opposition is in your face, take a deep breath and let it fly; and, finally, what Kurt Gunther taught us: when the game is on the line, keep your eye on the ball and follow through, and even if you are one of the smallest players on the field, you just might help deliver a miracle.

EPILOGUE—
WHERE ARE
THEY NOW?

The 1980 Holiday Bowl featured many players who would go on from that game to make names for themselves in the NFL. Some were drafted. Some signed free agent contracts and got tryouts with NFL, CFL, or USFL teams. Some never made rosters or made it off of practice squads, but others went on to enjoy lengthy, successful careers in the NFL. Still others have gone on to successful coaching careers. Some of the young players on the 1980 team would become star players for BYU over the next several years and be instrumental in closing out victories for BYU in subsequent Holiday Bowls from 1981 to 1984, including the national championship game. Though they lost to Ohio State in 1982, BYU defeated strong teams from major conferences in the 1981, '83, and '84 bowls. Each of those games were close, "nail biting" victories that came down to the final seconds before the outcome was decided. It is probably not a stretch to say that the lessons those young players observed and learned in the Miracle Bowl served them well when the chips were down in those later games. I have little doubt that in the final minutes of the '83 Missouri game and the '84 Michigan game, the players were buoyed up and encouraged by the memory of the team's impossible comeback in the 1980 game.

Several young players on the BYU roster that night went on to stellar careers in the NFL, most notably NFL Hall of Famer, Steve Young. After earning consensus all-American honors and finishing as the runner-up in the Heisman Trophy race, behind running back Mike Rozier of Nebraska and ahead of Doug Flutie of Boston College, Steve signed the famous forty million dollar deal with the Los Angeles Express of the USFL and then was the first pick in the 1984 Supplemental NFL draft by the Tampa Bay Buccaneers. He had an NFL Hall of Fame and NFL and Super Bowl MVP career with the San Francisco 49ers, after playing in the USFL and for the Buccaneers. Steve won the Davy O'Brien award as the best quarterback in college football and was inducted into the BYU Hall of Fame in 1994 and the College Football Hall of Fame in 2001.

If you look closely after Gunther's final kick, you can see Steve sprint on to the field and jump in jubilation at the victory (wearing jersey number 6). Steve played seventeen years in the USFL and NFL; won three NFL MVP awards; was all-pro three times; played in the Pro Bowl seven times; and was the record-setting Super Bowl MVP in Super Bowl XXIX. He was inducted into the Pro Football Hall of Fame in 2005. Steve graduated from BYU law school, works as an analyst and commentator for ESPN, is a successful venture capitalist, and is busy raising his four children in Northern California.

Gordon Hudson, who was also a freshman in 1980, and later a consensus all-American at BYU, was inducted into the College Football Hall of Fame in 2010. Gordon played in the USFL with Steve Young and for the Seattle Seahawks in the NFL, but injuries plagued him throughout his career, and he was never able to realize his potential in the NFL. Todd Shell, who played on special teams in Holiday Bowl III, went on to become a star linebacker at BYU, was drafted in the first round of the NFL draft, and played four seasons in the NFL with the San Francisco 49ers. He earned a Super Bowl ring with the Niners in 1984, along with former BYU players Bill Ring and Tom Holmoe.

Jim Herrmann became an all-WAC first team defensive lineman on BYU's national championship team in 1984 and was drafted in the seventh round of the NFL draft by the Dallas Cowboys. He also spent a season with the Cincinnati Bengals. Trevor Matich, who was a sophomore center on the 1980 team, left the program to serve a mission in Mexico and then returned to play for the Cougars in the 1983 and 1984 seasons. He was the all-WAC first team center on the national championship team and was drafted in the first round of the 1985 NFL draft by the New England Patriots. He played three seasons with the Patriots and a total of eleven seasons in the league with various teams. He is now a successful sports broadcaster with ESPN.

Freshman Vai Sikahema, who returned the SMU punt for a touchdown just before halftime, served a mission in South Dakota; went on

From left: Vai Sikahema (23), Scott Pettis (29)

to play eight seasons in the NFL for the Cardinals, Packers, and Eagles; made the Pro Bowl and became a successful sports personality and broadcaster in Philadelphia as a sports director and anchor. At BYU Vai was on the national championship team and earned all-WAC honors as a return specialist. He was inducted into the BYU Hall of Fame in 2002. In 2014 he was called as an LDS stake president in New Jersey.

In keeping with his fearless nature, in 2008 Vai made headlines again by accepting an offer to fight former professional baseball player Jose Canseco in a charity boxing match. The fight was over in less than two minutes as the 5' 9" 185-pound Sikahema thrashed the 6' 4" 240-pound Canseco. Canseco was knocked out by Vai a minute and a half into the first round. Vai, who had done a lot of boxing in his youth and who had been somewhat disrespected by Canseco before the fight, said he was only surprised it took him that long to knock Canseco out.

One memory that Vai has hung on to all of these years is from the locker room after the game. It involves then President Jeffrey Holland. Vai recalls, "Just as we gathered for the post-game prayer, President Holland said, "Men," with tears flowing down his cheeks, "among my many heroes are Joseph Smith, Winston Churchill, and Abraham Lincoln." He paused

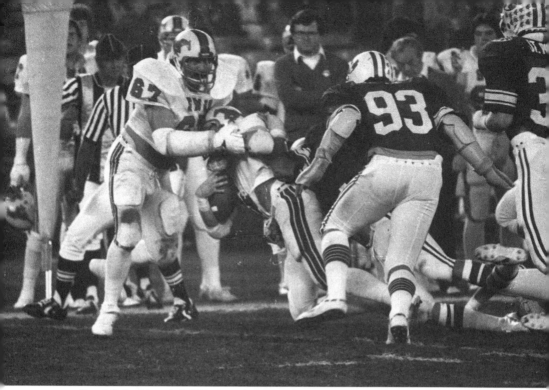

From left: Brad Anae (93), Ed St. Pierre (38)

briefly and scanned the room of young, sweaty faces. "For the rest of my life, I will add the 1980 BYU football team to that lofty list." Vai explains the reason that he remembers that so well is that he was holding President Holland's hand with one of his hands and fellow running back Scott Pettis's hand with his other hand.[1]

Vai's position as NBC anchor in Philadelphia has taken him all over the world covering sporting events, including Olympic games on nearly every continent. He says that no matter where he is, people will approach him and say something like, "Weren't you on the BYU Miracle Bowl team?" Vai also recalls that during the 1992 NFL season, when Jim McMahon and Vai both played for the Eagles, former SMU defensive back Wes Hopkins, who fought Clay Brown for the Hail Mary pass in the end zone, was also with the Eagles. Vai said there was a lot of banter that went back and forth about the Miracle Bowl. After one practice some of the other Eagles players—including the late, great Reggie White—convinced McMahon, Sikahema, and Hopkins that they should reenact the Hail Mary play with McMahon and Hopkins playing themselves and Sikahema taking Clay Brown's role in the play.

McMahon dropped back and launched the ball at the end zone as Hopkins and Sikahema cruised into the paint just as Brown, Hopkins,

From left: Scott Phillips (20), Scott Collie (3)

and others had done in 1980. As the ball arced toward the end zone, Sikahema realized that he was not 6' 3" like Brown and that Hopkins would be able to out jump him for the ball. So, as Hopkins gathered himself under the ball, Vai—ever the quick thinker—pulled Hopkins's shorts down to his knees and then out jumped him for the ball and another "miracle" touchdown. The other Eagles players roared with laughter at the spectacle.[2]

Sikahema also recalls that in his first Pro Bowl in 1986, he was on Eric Dickerson's NFC team. At one point, when Dickerson learned that Sikahema was from BYU, he jokingly complained that SMU had somehow been "cheated" in the loss of the 1980 Holiday Bowl. By that time it was pretty generally known that SMU had run afoul of the rules of the NCAA, so Sikahema responded, "Now that's funny—an SMU guy claiming that BYU cheated!"

Freshman Lee Johnson, who was the onside kicker in the bowl game and who was the punter and kicker on BYU's national championship team, had an eighteen-year career in the NFL as a kicker and punter. For a time he held the record for the most punts in NFL history over the course of his career with the Oilers, Browns, Bengals, Vikings, Eagles, and Patriots. Lee punted for the Bengals in Super Bowl XXIII and set a

Super Bowl record with a sixty-three yard punt, which was then returned for a touchdown by John Taylor of the 49ers. Ultimately the Bengals lost to the 49ers and Lee's good friend Steve Young.

Glen Titensor, who was an honorable mention all-American defensive end at BYU and an all–WAC first team member, was drafted in the third round of the 1981 NFL draft. He played seven seasons in the NFL as an offensive lineman for the Dallas Cowboys. Glen was from Westminster, California, and transferred to BYU from UCLA. He now lives with his family in the Dallas area, where he owns and operates a golf facility. Glen was named the defensive MVP of the Holiday Bowl by the Mizlou Television Network—although in many official Holiday Bowl publications, Jim McMahon and Craig James are identified as the MVPs of the game. When asked about his MVP status, Glen explains, "I've never told anyone I was the defensive MVP of the game. I don't want to be known as the defensive MVP in a game where there was no defense. That would mean I was the best of the worst!"[3]

Defensive lineman Chuck Ehin was a star on the BYU defensive line for two years and was drafted by the San Diego Chargers in the 1983 draft. He played five seasons for the Chargers. Defensive lineman Mike Morgan played for the Chicago Blitz and other teams in the USFL for three seasons and then returned to Utah, where he has been a high school football coach for many years. As part of his career, he spent thirteen seasons as the head football coach at West Jordan High School. Defensive lineman Brad Anae continued to play for BYU through the 1981 season, after transferring from the University of Hawaii. He earned all-WAC honors and signed as a free agent with the Philadelphia Eagles in 1982. He then played for several teams in the USFL.

Scott Collie, a back-up receiver on the 1980 Cougar team, went on to start for the Cougars the following two seasons. He played three seasons in the Canadian Football League for the Hamilton Tiger-Cats, and he also spent time with the San Francisco 49ers and the Denver Gold of the USFL. He played in two Grey Cup Championship games with Hamilton. Scott was baptized into the LDS church in 1979, and he and his wife, Nicole, have sent three sons, Zachary, Austin, and Dylan to BYU on football scholarships and on LDS missions. His son Austin was a consensus all-American receiver at BYU and was on the all-rookie team in the NFL with the Indianapolis Colts. Austin played for the Colts in Super Bowl XLIV (which they lost to the Saints) in his rookie season, spent four seasons with the Colts, and then played the 2013 season with the New England Patriots. Scott and his sons have launched a successful football coaching and consulting business called ReceiverTech, where they host camps and work with upcoming, young football players around the country.

Reserve offensive lineman Andy Reid has gone on to be a successful head coach in the NFL for many years, including a trip to the Super Bowl as head coach of the Philadelphia Eagles. He was baptized a member of the Church of Jesus Christ of Latter-day Saints after transferring to BYU from Glendale Community College in 1978. Andy is now the head coach

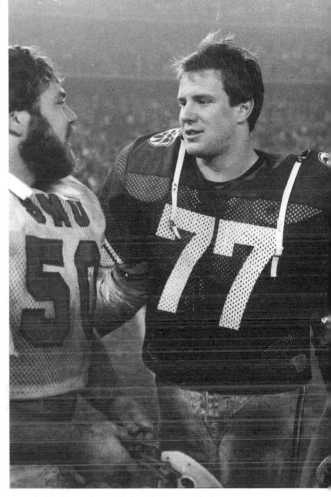

From left: Lance Pederson (50), Mike Morgan (77)

of the Kansas City Chiefs, and he took the team to the playoffs in his first season. Andy and his wife, Tammy, whom he married while at BYU, recall being inspired by the Miracle Bowl win during two memorable come-from-behind victories they had while in Philadelphia—known as Miracle in the Meadowlands II and III.

Tom Holmoe, who was on the WAC all-academic team in 1980 and led the league with seven interceptions, continued to star for BYU until after the 1982 season, in which he earned all-WAC honors. He was drafted by the San Francisco 49ers in the fourth round of the 1983 draft, played seven seasons for the 49ers and won three Super Bowl rings with them. He coached at BYU, Stanford, and the University of California. In 1994 he was the defensive backs coach for the 49ers when they won the Super Bowl behind Steve Young's six-touchdown-pass MVP performance and

Tom earned a fourth Super Bowl ring for that game. He married BYU cheerleader Lori Wright in 1982 and was baptized in 1988. Tom is now the athletic director at BYU.

BYU defensive back Bill Schoepflin earned honorable mention all-America honors and was named to the all–Western Athletic Conference first team for the 1980 season. He signed with the Ottawa Rough Riders of the Canadian Football league but was cut due to the restrictions on the numbers of US players that could be signed by teams in the CFL. He then got a tryout with the Baltimore Colts in the NFL. It appeared Bill was going to make that team until he dislocated his hip and tore ligaments in his knee during a goal line stand in one of the final pre-season games against the Washington Redskins. Those injuries ended his football career.

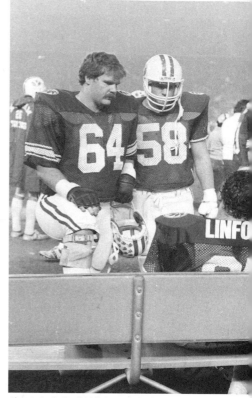

Above: Andy Reid (64), Vince Stroth (58), Ray Linford (67)
Opposite top: Bill Schoepflin (43)
Opposite bottom: Lee Johnson (16), Tom Holmoe (46), Kevin Walker (14)

Bill was really the unsung hero for BYU in the Miracle Bowl. He played well throughout game, but in the last half-minute of the game he made three crucial plays that helped secure the comeback—and two of the plays set the table for the Hail Mary play. First he stopped Eric Dickerson short of first-down yardage on SMU's last offensive play and forced them to punt. If Dickerson had made the first down, SMU would have won the game. Then, Schoepflin blocked the SMU punt to put the ball back in McMahon's hands for the final few plays and the Hail Mary. Finally, Bill calmly took the late snap on the extra point and got it down just in the nick of time for Gunther to score the final winning point. McMahon and Brown justifiably received much attention for their role in the comeback, but without Schoepflin's tackle on Dickerson followed by the blocked punt, the Hail Mary play would never have happened.

Top: Ed St. Pierre (38)
Bottom, from left: Kyle Whittingham (59), Bob Prested (5)

Bill married a girl from Provo, Utah, and they settled in the Denver, Colorado, area where he served for many years as a police officer in Arvada, Colorado. Bill and his wife, Tracy, raised their children in the LDS Church and Bill was baptized in 2009. Bill and Tracy have now been sealed in the LDS Temple.

Starting strong safety Mark Brady earned all-WAC honors at BYU and after graduation he coached football at Weber State College, Utah State University, and for the Birmingham Thunderbolts in the XFL. Mark and his wife Karin raised eight children and now reside in St. George, Utah, where they are involved in various business interests. Mark's identical twin brother, Steve, who was a reserve safety on the 1980 BYU team, gained some notoriety of his own during the bowl game for a hit he laid on the SMU kicker, Eddie Garcia, after a kick-off. Garcia turned just as Steve got to him so Steve hit him in the back and leveled him. Steve did not intend to hit Garcia that way and offered his hand to help him up, but Garcia was upset and angrily knocked Steve's extended hand away. It was all reviewed on the television in close-up slow motion as the announcers laughed about what they were seeing.

Ed St. Pierre, one of the starting BYU linebackers, was baptized into the LDS church and has sent children back to BYU. Bob Prested was a three-year starter at free safety and one of the leaders in defensive statistics for the 1980 season. Wide receiver Lloyd Jones was drafted by the New York Jets in the eighth round of the 1981 draft. He also played in the USFL. Sadly, Lloyd passed away a few years ago.

Bart Oates was the starting center for BYU in the Holiday Bowl and went on star for BYU for two more years. Then he had a long and successful career in the USFL and NFL, including five trips to the NFL Pro Bowl. He was twice voted all-pro. He was a unanimous choice for the NFL all-Rookie team in 1985. At BYU he was two-time academic all-WAC, was named to the WAC all-decade team, and played in all the major post-season all star games after his senior season. He was inducted into the BYU Hall of Fame in 1992. He won two championships with the Baltimore/Philadelphia Stars of the USFL. He also won two Super Bowls with the Giants and one with the 49ers in 1994 when Steve Young was the MVP quarterback.

Bart went on to graduate from Seton-Hall law school and is a now a successful businessman in New Jersey. Following the Miracle Bowl game Oates returned to Provo and stayed there with his parents during the holidays when most students had left the area. He asked out a local girl that he had had his eyes on for a while, and they spent nearly every waking moment together during the holidays. Bart now explains that "due to the euphoria" created by the Holiday Bowl victory, he had the courage to ask her to marry him just before they returned to school after the holiday break. He explains, "We became engaged after about a week of dating, and now Michelle has been my wife for over thirty years. I had just participated in one miracle, so why not another one?"[4]

The 1994 Super Bowl win for the 49ers was especially interesting to me, and not just because Steve Young was the quarterback and Bart Oates was his center. Earlier in the year, *Sports Illustrated* magazine had published a lengthy report wherein it had concluded that the closer a player lines up to the ball, the more intelligent that player needs to be. In other words, a center needs to be smarter than guards, guards smarter than tackles, quarterbacks need to be smarter than other backs and so forth. After I read that article, I wrote a letter to the SI Editor, which was printed in the October 3, 1994, issue of the magazine (the issue that coincidently featured the University of Colorado Miracle at Michigan Hail Mary play on the cover).

In that letter I argued that if the conclusion about smarter players lining up closer to the ball was valid, the 49ers should be shoo-ins to win

From left: Lloyd Jones (87), Coach Edwards

the Super Bowl that year. I pointed out that the center, Oates, and the quarterback, Young, were both law school graduates, and they were the only two 49ers who would touch the ball on every offensive play. That somewhat tongue-in-cheek letter to the editor ended up being an accurate prediction of the Super Bowl winner that year.

Offensive linemen Calvin Close and Nick Eyre both played for a year or two in the NFL, with the Saints and Oilers, respectively. Eyre, a fourth-round draft pick of the Oilers, was a first team all-American in 1980 and was third in the Outland Trophy voting. He also played in the USFL but was forced to retire after being diagnosed with Hodgkin's disease. Nick, who did not have much to do with the LDS Church while he was at BYU, was sealed in the LDS temple in 1987. Close was honorable mention all-American and all–Western Athletic Conference first team and he was named to the 1980s all-decade team. Calvin and his family settled in Salt Lake City where he has worked for many years as a media account executive.

Calvin recalls that his parents attended the Holiday Bowl in San Diego, having driven down from their home in Camarillo, California. However, like many others, they left the stadium when the score was 45–25 and were in the parking lot when they heard the cheering from the final play. Not realizing that the cheering was for BYU, they did not learn that BYU had rallied to win the game until later on that night.

Reserve tight end Rob Anderson played for the Los Angeles Rams for a couple of years. Offensive lineman Ray Linford—who had followed his older brother, Paul, to BYU as an offensive lineman—passed away in 2005.

Corey Pace graduated in 1982 with a business degree and settled in Southern California where he and his wife, Marsha, whom he married the morning after Holiday Bowl III, raised their family and own an engineering company. Corey laughs when he recalls that when they got to the Los Angeles LDS Temple at the appointed time the morning after the game, the wedding was delayed because many people in the temple wanted to talk about and celebrate the Miracle Bowl victory. Corey's son John was a long snapper for the Cougars from 2007–09. Corey was in the new Dallas Cowboys Stadium on September 5, 2009, watching his son long snap for BYU when the twentieth-ranked Cougars beat third-ranked Oklahoma 14–13. It was the first college game played in that new stadium and another significant victory for BYU.

Left: Calvin Close (63); Right: Dan Plater (86)

After his senior season at BYU in 1981, where he was named academic all-American and MVP of the East-West Shrine game, receiver Dan Plater was drafted by the Denver Broncos in the fourth round, making him a teammate of Clay Brown's. But he was the last player cut by the Broncos that pre-season and was then picked up by the Chicago Bears to team up, once again, with Jim McMahon. Plater, who had been McMahon's favorite target at BYU, was on the roster of the 1985 Super Bowl Champion Bears at the beginning of the season, but his career was cut short by a brain tumor that had to be surgically removed. McMahon famously wore a headband with Plater's nickname "Pluto" on it during the playoff run that year to honor his receiver and friend, who was recovering from brain surgery at the time.

Receiver Matt Braga graduated from BYU in the spring of 1981 with a business degree. Matt was second team all–Western Athletic Conference, and he got a brief tryout with the Tampa Bay Buccaneers from legendary Green Bay Packer receiver Boyd Dowler. Dowler was working as a scout for Tampa Bay at the time. During that workout it was discovered that a knee injury Matt had received earlier in the 1980 season was in actuality a torn ACL ligament that needed to be surgically repaired. That discovery and subsequent surgery effectively ended Matt's football career. Matt and his wife Jayne, who attended BYU with Matt, have raised their two kids in Southern California. He has worked for many years in the medical devices business.

It was fortunate that Braga was able to play in the 1980 Holiday Bowl at all. In one of the first workouts in San Diego, Braga's injured knee popped out and, as a result, he was only able to get in some jogging and physical therapy during the rest of the week. He was unable to participate in full practices with the team, and it was reported that he had suffered a knee "extension." Finally, his knee was drained, which gave him some mobility for the game, and he was able to play. Trainer Marv Roberson "did a great job" taping up Braga's torn ACL knee and, "I was ready to go on game day,"[5] recalled Matt.

Running back Scott Phillips earned several honors in 1980, including academic all-America first team. He was drafted by the Seattle Seahawks in the fourth round of the 1981 draft and spent some time with the New York Giants too. Injuries hampered his efforts to land on an NFL roster. He married BYU cheerleader Linda Madsen, graduated from BYU law school, and is now a successful insurance and estate planning professional in Utah.

Running back Eric Lane, who was honorable mention all–Western Athletic Conference, was drafted by the Seattle Seahawks and played seven NFL seasons in Seattle, where he was their special teams captain. Reserve running back Blair Buswell, who had a successful career as a running back at Ricks College and was attending BYU on an art scholarship, graduated in 1982 and has become a world-renowned sculptor and artist. He has sculpted over eighty busts for NFL players who have been inducted into the NFL Pro Football Hall of Fame, including his BYU teammate Steve Young. Blair also sculpted Jack Nicklaus for the Georgia Golf Hall of Fame and John Wooden for the Pauley Pavilion in Los Angeles. And he sculpted the Doak Walker Award, named after the 1940s SMU player, which is given annually to the best running back in college football. In a bit of irony, Blair was also commissioned to sculpt the NFL Hall of Fame bust of Eric Dickerson. Blair has great memories of his interaction with Dickerson. They spent several days together so Blair could make measurements and prepare to do the sculpting.

He told Eric that he was on the 1980 BYU team. Blair explains, "At that point, our meeting turned into a trash talk fest as we each took up our positions about the outcome of the game."

Dickerson argued that BYU won the game on lucky plays. "How about that lucky punt return at the end of the first half?"

Blair responded, "What do you mean lucky? That was Vai Sikahema who was an NFL Pro Bowl returner."

"That was Vai?" Dickerson knew of Vai from the NFL but didn't realize he had returned the punt for BYU. Then Dickerson mentioned the "lucky" onside kick.

Blair responded, "You mean Lee Johnson?"

"That was Lee?"

And so it went.

Years later Blair ran into 1980 SMU coach Ron Meyer at the Doak Walker Award Ceremony where Dickerson and James were being awarded a legacy award. Blair introduced himself and mentioned he had been on the 1980 BYU team. Meyer groaned and took Blair over to meet Dickerson and James. Dickerson rolled his eyes and said, "I already know this guy!"[6]

Offensive lineman Lloyd Eldredge played for BYU through the 1982 season and earned all-WAC honors his senior year. After he graduated from BYU with a degree in finance, Lloyd flew F-16 fighters in the US Air Force and became the Air Force's version of a "Top Gun" pilot and an instructor. He is now a captain with Delta Airlines. Lloyd and his wife have six children, including two children they adopted from Russia. One of Lloyd's poignant memories from the game occurred late in the third quarter when it appeared that the game would be won by SMU. Lloyd was still playing hard, trying his best to stop the onslaught of the SMU defensive rush. For much of the game, Lloyd had lined up opposite one of the SMU defensive stars, Harvey Armstrong. Armstrong was a 255-pound wrecking machine and he had played an outstanding game. As they lined up for a play, Lloyd recalls that Armstrong leaned over a little and said, "Why don't y'all ease up a bit, the game's over?"[7] Of course, that did not have the desired effect on Lloyd, who kept pounding away the remainder of the game.

Kyle Whittingham was first team all-WAC in 1981 and was named the WAC Defensive Player of the Year. He played in the USFL and the NFL and has made a name for himself as the head coach of the University of Utah Utes. In 2008 he nearly won a national championship when his Utes beat up on the famed Alabama Crimson Tide in the Sugar Bowl and finished with a perfect 13-0 record. Utah and Coach Whittingham

Top: Matt Braga (19)
Bottom: Scott Phillips (20)

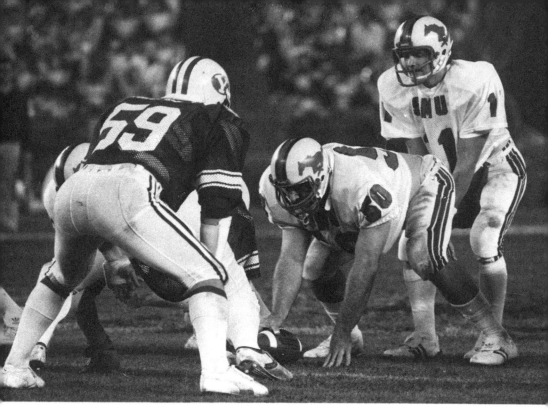

Kyle Whittingham (59)

certainly had a legitimate claim that they should have been the national champions that year rather than the 13-1 Florida Gators.

My roommate at the 1980 Holiday Bowl, reserve quarterback Gym Kimball, left BYU after the 1981 season and transferred to Utah State University where he was the starting quarterback for the Aggies for more or less two seasons and passed for nearly 2000 yards in 1984. He earned a free agent tryout with the Dallas Cowboys and ended up in business in Salt Lake City. Kimball and his Aggies did not fare too well when they visited Cougar Stadium in late November 1984. They were up against the undefeated, number-one-ranked, and soon-to-be-national-champion Cougars. Although Gym threw for 274 yards and one touchdown as the starting USU quarterback, BYU—behind a two-touchdown effort by Vai Sikahema—won the game 38 to 13 in front of nearly 66,000 fans. It was the largest crowd to watch the Cougars play that championship season— including when they went up against Michigan in the Holiday Bowl.

I attended the BYU–USU game and went down on the field after the game to say hello to Gym. He was bloodied, muddied, and bruised, but had retained his sense of humor. A year or two later, Gym organized a Salt Lake County recreation flag football team that included some of his former Skyline High School and Utah State teammates and me. We played together for several seasons and won a championship one year against a team loaded up with former players from the University of Utah.

After earning a scholarship for his kicking during the 1980 season, Kurt Gunther continued to kick for BYU for two more seasons and graduated with a degree in accounting. He earned all-WAC honorable mention and was academic all-WAC and all-district. Kurt has worked in accounting and financial services for years in Utah County and surrounding areas. Kurt said, "You can't believe the mileage I have gotten out of one kick. People still come up to me and ask me about that game and kick."[8] Inexplicably, in the 1981 BYU football press guide, where a player's accomplishments are highlighted in their player bios, there is no mention of Kurt's game-winning kick in Holiday Bowl III.

Kurt had a very successful run as a kicker for BYU, scoring 243 points in his three varsity seasons. His points were instrumental in winning several games, such as the game against the University of Hawaii in 1981 when Kurt scored 7 of BYU's 13 points in a 13 to 3 victory. But, when it comes to last-minute or no-time-left kicks to win a game, the only two opportunities Kurt had were the 1979 Snow College JV game and the 1980 Holiday-Bowl-winning kick. And he made them both.

Clay Brown was drafted by the Denver Broncos in the second round of the 1981 draft and played a few years for the Broncos and Falcons. Brown is now a successful businessman living in Arizona. In 1999 Brown was inducted into the BYU Hall of Fame. It is no secret that his catch of the Hail Mary pass in the Miracle Bowl was a significant factor in Brown's induction. The football he caught for that final touchdown and his Holiday Bowl jersey are proudly on display in Cougar Legacy Hall at the BYU football headquarters, courtesy of Brown.

After Brown's catch, the ball was retrieved by Floyd Johnson, who kept the ball, knowing that it would have historical significance. Sometime later Floyd gave the ball and some other BYU memorabilia to a young friend and neighbor named Mark Gowans. Years later, after Floyd had passed away, Mr. Gowans saw an interview with Clay Brown where Clay was asked if he could go back to that night in San Diego Stadium and change anything what would he change. Clay's response was that he would not hand the ball to the official after the touchdown, he would keep it. Clay gave the ball to the referee because he had to get ready to block for the extra point.

Clay Brown (85)

Mr. Gowans looked up Clay at the BYU game the next day and said, "I have something I want to give you." They got together and Mr. Gowans said he had the miracle catch ball and wanted Clay to have it. An exchange of the ball was arranged through the university athletic department, and Clay and his family accepted the gift from Mr. Gowans during half time at a subsequent BYU game in Provo. Brown then loaned the famous—if not magical—ball to BYU to be put on display in Legacy Hall. A close inspection of the ball today reveals faded initials on the ball, "M.G." for Mark Gowans. Clay is still moved by Mr. Gowans's generosity in returning the ball to him.[9]

McMahon and Brown are well deserving of any and all accolades that have been made about their performance in that game, and not just the Hail Mary play. Brown scored three touchdowns in the game, all on passes from McMahon. After the Hail Mary pass, McMahon hugged Brown as part of the celebration and told him he was the best tight end in the land. The thirty-plus years of fame generated by that catch continue to confirm McMahon's statement; Brown really was the best tight end in the collegiate game that year.

Jim McMahon was a two-time all-American at BYU; won the Davey O'Brien Award and the Sammy Baugh Trophy (for the best passer and quarterback in the college game, respectively); and was third in the Heisman trophy voting, behind running backs Marcus Allen (USC) and Herschel Walker (Georgia) in 1981. Jim ended up fifth in the Heisman vote in 1980—before Holiday Bowl III. He finished behind George Rogers of South Carolina; Hugh Green of Pittsburg; Herschel Walker of Georgia; and another quarterback, Mark Herrmann of Purdue University. One wonders how the votes for Jim would have turned out that year if they were cast after the Miracle Bowl. Following another stellar performance in his senior year at BYU, including another nail-biting win in the 1981 Holiday Bowl, Jim was the fifth pick in the first round of the 1982 NFL draft. He was drafted by the Chicago Bears.

Jim McMahon's exploits in the NFL are well known. He became the starter for the Bears in his rookie season and was named NFC Rookie of the Year. As predicted by Coach Edwards, within a few years McMahon led his Chicago Bears to a 15 and 1 record and a Super Bowl blowout against New England. In that game McMahon would, once again, beat former SMU running back Craig James in a bowl game. James had been a star for the Patriots in their run to the Super Bowl. But in the Super Bowl, McMahon scored two running touchdowns and guided the Bears to a lopsided 46–10 victory. McMahon and his Bears also defeated Eric Dickerson and his Los Angeles Rams as they tried to make it to the Super Bowl that season. The Bears pummeled the Rams 24–0 in the NFC championship game. The Bears's defense held Dickerson to just 46 rushing yards. McMahon scored on a 16-yard run and threw a 22-yard touchdown pass.

The Patriots beat the Oakland Raiders in the divisional playoff round by a touchdown and then advanced to play the Bears in the Super Bowl in New Orleans. If Oakland had made it to the Super Bowl, as many had predicted they would, the Super Bowl would have featured two former BYU quarterbacks and teammates starting against each other: Jim McMahon for the Bears and Marc Wilson for the Raiders. That would have been exciting for Cougar fans to watch and probably would have been a better game than the Bears' smackdown of the Patriots and their largely ineffective quarterbacks during that game. At the time I recall being very disappointed that McMahon and Wilson did not face each other in that Super Bowl. (Wilson did receive two Super Bowl rings as a backup quarterback for the Raiders in 1980 and 1984.)

McMahon became known as the "Punky QB" and gained much notoriety for tweaking NFL Commissioner Pete Rozelle with "headband gate" and for showing his backside to a circling press helicopter at a Bears practice session during Super Bowl week to "show them where it hurts." McMahon played in the NFL for fifteen seasons with six different teams and won two Super Bowl rings—with the Bears in Super Bowl XX, as the starter, and with the Packers in Super Bowl XXXI as Brett Favre's backup. Jim played in the Pro Bowl and was voted all-pro in 1985. Throughout his career he was a unique sports personality, starring in several crazy television commercials, the "Super Bowl Shuffle" music video, and other such campaigns. Jim was featured on the cover of *Sports Illustrated* many times, including the December 1991 issue touting him as the "Masked Marvel" with his tinted visor on his Philadelphia Eagles helmet.

More recently Jim has been in the news for being one of the lead plaintiffs in a lawsuit against the NFL regarding concussions and dementia. Jim was on the cover of *Sports Illustrated* magazine in 2012, dealing with the issues he faces in his life because of the injuries he sustained while playing in the NFL.

In 2010 McMahon returned to BYU as part of quarterback weekend, when the school honored its many all-American signal-callers. McMahon was greeted by BYU fans with what many thought was the loudest ovation of the day. In the fall of 2011, Roy High School in Utah retired Jim's jersey number and welcomed their favorite son back for halftime festivities at a Royals football game. Coach Edwards and a few BYU teammates attended the game to honor Jim and his many accomplishments. I hadn't seen Jim in many years, but he greeted me like I was part of his family—a trait that Jim always exhibited to his teammates, even those who were not stars. That is one of the characteristics that made Jim's teammates rally around him. In 2014 Jim was inducted into the Utah Sports Hall of Fame—along with Billy Casper, Marv Fleming, Ron McBride and Michele Fellows-Lewis. In the early fall of 2014, Jim completed his course work at BYU and obtained his degree. In accordance with BYU policy, it was then announced that Jim was eligible to be inducted in to the BYU Hall of Fame. When Jim informed me he had graduated, he used his typical deadpan humor to downplay the accomplishment. He exclaimed, "I don't know what the big deal is, it only took me thirty-seven years!"

On October 2nd and 3rd, 2014, Jim was inducted into the BYU Sports Hall Fame and had his jersey retired and displayed from the top of LaVell Edwards stadium, along with other BYU football stars of the past.

In an article that ran in the *Deseret News* on October 2, 2014, Vai Sikahema defended BYU's decision to induct Jim and retire his jersey by recounting Jim's amazing records on the field and then recounting a few of the unknown acts of charity and kindness that Jim has shown to former teammates over the years, such as paying for their stays in treatment facilities and supporting them in other ways, all quietly and without any fanfare. In that article, Vai also quotes a tutor, Trevor Wilson, who helped

Jim finish off his course work in order to receive his degree:

> Jim McMahon accomplished something greater than any game, any "Hail Mary," and any Super Bowl season. Jim overcame not just a disability, but a stereotype often given to nonmember athletes who don't fit the square peg—he got a degree.

And to show that Jim still has the same fire that burned so brightly in San Diego on that December night in San Diego, Mr. Wilson further explains:

> Jim talked with me about the reasons why he wants to graduate. The roots stem from a promise he made his father that he would complete his degree.

Jim McMahon (9) and his father

He also talked about wanting to finish something he started. As an educator for over twenty years, I have preached to thousands of people (youths) the importance of an education, mostly based on the opportunities it brings for the future. I learned from Jim something deeper; an education meant accomplishing something that represents a challenge. Conquering a mountain you once began to climb and promised people you would. Jim doesn't need a degree for money. I don't even think he feels he has to be in the BYU Hall of Fame. I think Jim wants a piece of paper on his wall in his office that sits right next to the hundreds of athletic awards he has won (including a Super Bowl) that right now means more to him than all the others because it was accomplished with his mind—a college degree.

Fighting through the injuries and limitations his long football career left him with, Jim once again refused to punt; he refused to come off of the field until he had the victory.

Linebacker Glen Redd, who was honorable mention all-American and all–Western Athletic Conference first team, was drafted by the New

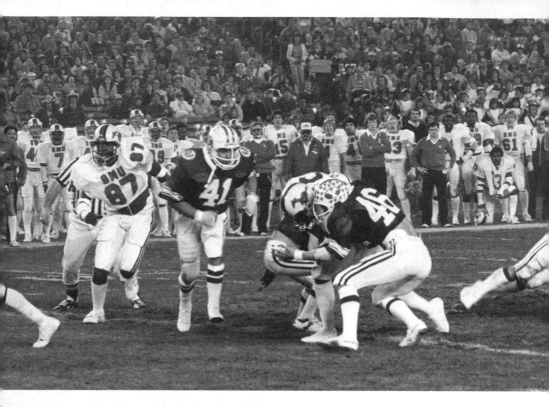

Above, from left: Glen Redd (41), Tom Holmoe (46)
Left, from left: Scott Phillips (20), Bill Davis (88), Dan Plater (86)

Orleans Saints in the sixth round of the 1981 draft, started every game as a rookie, and played five seasons for the Saints and one for the Colts. He led the Saints in tackles in 1981 and 1985. Sadly, Glen passed away after a battle with cancer in 2007. Glen, who was a tough-as-nails and hard hitting linebacker, was noted in his obituary as one who was known for his service to others and his love of the Savior. His obituary also proudly declares: "Glen anchored the defense in the amazing game now referred to as 'The 1980 Miracle Bowl.'"

Ty Mattingly, who was a freshman defensive lineman on the 1980 team, recalls a touching exchange he had with Glen Redd a few years before Glen passed away—relating to an incident that occurred on the BYU sidelines during the 1980 Holiday Bowl. Ty was dressed in his game uniform, but, as the game progressed, he put on the large, decorated cowboy hats that had been given to all of the players for the game and were part of the official Holiday Bowl clothing package.

At some point in the game, when things were not going well for the Cougars and emotions were running hot, Redd saw Ty in the cowboy hat, standing on the sidelines. Redd approached Ty and yelled at him to take the stupid cowboy hat off and get his head in the game if he was going to stand with the team on the sidelines. Ty was shocked at Redd's reaction to him, since he was a freshman who would likely not play in the game, but he did remove the hat and then simply avoided Redd. Ty also recalls that he thought it was strange that Redd would be focused on the cowboy hat given the disaster that was unfolding on the field, but that story just highlights the confusion and frustration that permeated the team at the low points of the game.

Ty explains, "I just had nothing to do with Redd after that and didn't really see or talk to him for twenty-three years." Then, at Coach Whittingham's funeral in 2003, Ty was standing at one end of the large cultural hall where the funeral was held and he saw Glen Redd come in and yell across the hall, "Ty Mattingly" as Redd rushed toward him.

Ty thought, "Oh no, here we go again; what is he going to scream at me about now?"

Glen walked up to Ty and said, "There is something I've been wanting to say to you for over twenty years now." Glen then recounted his blowup on the sidelines at the Holiday Bowl that night and profusely apologized to Ty, admitting he was out of line with his heated rant that night in San Diego. Ty was very grateful to hear those words from Glen, accepted his apology, and gained much respect for Glen and his humility (and memory). The whole affair, of course, meant even more to Ty a few years later when Glen passed away too.

Back-up linebacker David Aupiu became a starter for BYU and played during the 1987 NFL strike season with the Los Angeles Rams. David passed away in 2010. Reserve defensive back Mike Jensen, who made a key tackle on a kickoff in the bowl game, became a successful physician. He has been involved in humanitarian work in the medical field with Doctors Without Borders and as team doctor for the Special Olympics. He passed away in 2012.

Receiver Bill Davis, a Baptist, who had several key receptions in the game—including the forty-yard reception where the officials called him out at the one-foot line late in the game—was honorable mention all-WAC and WAC all-academic in 1980. He graduated from BYU with a degree in geologic engineering and then received a degree in petroleum engineering from the University of Texas. He became a petroleum engineer and lived and worked in various places around the world. He last worked in Kuwait City, Kuwait, where he was tragically killed in an automobile accident in 2010.

SMU also had many players who had long careers in the NFL. Of course, Eric Dickerson is an NFL Hall of Fame running back who played for the Colts, Rams, Raiders, and Falcons and still holds the single-season rushing record of 2104 yards. He played eleven seasons in the NFL. Craig James, Dickerson's Pony Express running mate at SMU, played for the Washington Federals in the USFL and then with the New England Patriots in the NFL for four seasons. James made the Pro Bowl in 1986 and went on to a career as a sportscaster for ABC and ESPN.

Defensive linemen Harvey Armstrong and Michael Carter also had lengthy NFL careers. Armstrong played eight seasons with the Eagles and the Colts; Carter spent eight seasons with the 49ers, where he went to three Pro Bowls and won three Super Bowl rings. Carter also won a silver medal in the 1984 Los Angeles Olympics for the shot put. He still holds the US high school shot put record. SMU's kicker Eddie Garcia played two years in the NFL with the Green Bay Packers. John Simmons recovered from his shoulder injury; was drafted by the Bengals in the third round of the 1981 NFL draft; and played seven seasons as a defensive back in the NFL with the Bengals, Packers, and Colts.

Quarterback Lance McIlhenny, the outstanding option quarterback at SMU, and a freshman in 1980, became one of the most successful quarterbacks in Southwest Conference history, posting a career record of 34-5-1. Following football he pursued a career in commercial real estate and still lives in the Dallas area. He has never left his SMU roots. It was said of him that unlike many of his Mustang teammates, he did not leave the program but "stayed around for the funeral."

Wes Hopkins, the SMU safety who battled Brown for control of McMahon's last-second Hail Mary bomb, was drafted in the second round of the 1983 draft by the Philadelphia Eagles and played eleven years with them. Hopkins made the Pro Bowl and was considered one of the hardest-hitting safeties in the league.

Lee Spivey, an offensive tackle for SMU, was drafted by the Detroit Lions in 1981.

SMU defensive back Reggie Phillips, who was covering Matt Braga on Braga's diving touchdown catch, played four seasons in the NFL and was Jim McMahon's teammate on the Bears. Reggie was part of the famous "Super Bowl Shuffle" video and intercepted a Steve Grogan pass and returned it for a touchdown in the Super Bowl, helping to seal the Bears's blowout victory over the Patriots.

Linebacker Byron Hunt was drafted by the New York Giants in the 1981 draft and played eight seasons with them, winning a Super Bowl ring in 1986.

In 1982, Head Coach Ron Meyer left SMU (then under one order of probation and still being heavily investigated by the NCAA) and took the head coaching position with the New England Patriots. He had a somewhat turbulent run with the Patriots and was fired in 1984. He was replaced by Raymond Berry, who took the Patriots to the Super Bowl the next year to face Jim McMahon and the Bears. Meyer became a successful head coach for the Indianapolis Colts and was named AFC Coach of the Year in 1987. But things deteriorated over the next few years, and he was fired in 1991 after beginning the season 0-5. Since then he has held various coaching positions in the CFL and XFL, and as a football analyst.

Coach Meyer was a vocal supporter of BYU in 1984 when there were many critics of BYU's schedule and the national championship: "They do a tremendous job and they're a legitimate No. 1—that's all. They're sound. And they're a class, class operation. They've done it and I don't care who it's been against."[10]

APPENDIX

GAME LESSONS

GAME LESSON # 1: NEVER SAY "IMPOSSIBLE"

Small in body only, team manager Mel Farr tears a five-inch-thick San Diego telephone book in half with his bare hands to inspire and motivate the team. It almost makes him pass out, but he succeeds in this impossible task.

GAME LESSON #2: SOMETIMES WHEN THINGS LOOK HOPELESS, TAKE A RISK AND RUN LIKE YOU HAVE NOTHING TO LOSE

Freshman return specialist Vai Sikahema, realizing that something drastic is needed to wake up the Cougars, lets an SMU punt bounce as though he will let it die, and then—at great risk—he grabs the ball and sprints 83 yards for a BYU touchdown. McMahon tells Vai, "Kid, you just gave us a chance."

GAME LESSON #3: TEST THE OPPOSITION'S VULNERABILITIES AND THEN EXPLOIT THEM

Near the end of the first half, Bill Schoepflin comes within inches of blocking an SMU punt. He files that information away to be used later—with great success.

GAME LESSON # 4: NEVER, NEVER, NEVER GIVE UP

At a time in the fourth quarter when it looked like the game was over and lost, BYU quarterback Jim McMahon refuses to allow the team to punt and thereby give up on the game. He calls an audible, gets the first down, and then takes the team down the field for a score. His refusal to throw in the towel turns the momentum in BYU's favor.

GAME LESSON # 5: SOMETIMES SUCCESS COMES IF YOU DIVE AT A PROBLEM AND HANG ON UNTIL THE DUST CLEARS

Sprinting across the end zone, receiver Matt Braga lays out in a dive for a McMahon pass. He gets one arm on the ball and flips it to his chest. After sliding and rolling along the turf at full speed, he jumps up with the ball firmly in his grasp for a touchdown, but he's not really sure how the ball got there.

GAME LESSON #6: LEARN TO TRUST YOURSELF

After completely botching an onside kick, freshman Lee Johnson had no interest in trying another one. His coach angrily sends him back into the game to try another one at a very critical point in the game. In that tense situation, Lee executes a perfect onside kick, BYU recovers the ball, and within a few plays scores another touchdown.

GAME LESSON # 7: WANT IT MORE THAN THOSE TRYING TO STOP YOU

With no time on the clock, tight end Clay Brown fights off three or four SMU defenders and comes down with McMahon's 60-yard Hail Mary pass in the end zone for a touchdown. Amazed that Brown caught it, the announcers exclaimed, "He just seemed to want it!"

GAME LESSON # 8: WHEN THE GAME IS ON THE LINE, KEEP YOUR
EYE ON THE BALL AND FOLLOW THROUGH!

With the score tied at 45 to 45 and the game clock at :00, BYU kicker
Kurt Gunther ignores several distractions and problems and remembers
the lessons he learned from his mentor the year before. He follows his
fundamentals and wins the game with an extra point.

GAME LESSON #9: WHEN OPPOSITION IS IN YOUR FACE, TAKE A DEEP
BREATH AND LET IT FLY

For the game-winning extra-point snap, 230-pound Corey Pace
knew that as soon as he snapped the ball, he would get hammered by 265-
pound Michael Carter. Needing to calm down a bit from the miraculous
Hail Mary play before he snapped the ball, Pace took an extra second
to take a deep breath, and then he made a perfect rifle-shot snap for the
game-winning extra point.

1980 BYU ROSTER

No.	Name	Pos.	Ht.	Wt.	Class	Hometown
93	Brad Anae*	DE	6-4	229	Jr.	Laie, Hawaii
57	Robert Anae	C	6-5	227	Fr.	Laie, Hawaii
80	Rob Andersen**	TE	6-3½	230	Sr.	Salt Lake City, Utah
44	David Aupiu*	LB	6-2½	226	So.	Carson, California
89	Neil Balholm (redshirt)	WR	6-0½	175	Jr.	Vancouver, Washington
12	Mark Brady*	DB	6-0	180	Jr.	Oak Ridge, Tennessee
13	Steve Brady	DB	6-0	182	Jr.	Oak Ridge, Tennessee
19	Matt Braga*	WR	6-0	171	Sr.	Redlands, California
85	Clay Brown**	TE	6-3	222	Sr.	San Gabriel, California
10	Royce Bybee*	QB	6-2	185	Sr.	Alhambra, California
28	Pat Cabulagan (redshirt)	DB	6-1	165	So.	National City, California
30	Steve Carlsen*	FB	6-0	208	Sr.	Paris, Idaho
63	Calvin Close*	OT	6-3	225	Jr.	Camarillo, California
3	Scott Collie*	WR	6-1	190	So.	San Jose, California
88	Bill Davis**	WR	6-2	180	Sr.	Denver, Colorado
78	Chuck Ehin*	DT	6-3½	250	So.	Layton, Utah
56	Lloyd Eldredge*	OG	6-5	220	So.	Salt Lake City, Utah
72	Nick Eyre***	OT	6-5	276	Sr.	Las Vegas, Nevada
75	Wayne Faalafua	OT	6-3	266	So.	Carson, California
99	Brandon Flint	DE	6-5	237	So.	Layton, Utah
8	Dave Francis**	DB	5-11	185	Sr.	Salt Lake City, Utah
2	Kurt Gunther	K	5-10	170	So.	Provo, Utah
	Larry Hamilton	OT	6-4½	222	Fr.	Oxnard, California
33	Waymon Hamilton	FB	6-0	211	Fr.	Calipatria, California
34	Bruce Hansen	TB	6-0	208	Fr.	American Fork, Utah
84	Brad Hardisty	TE	6-6	200	So.	Las Vegas, Nevada
	Adam Haysbert	WR	5-11½	173	Fr.	San Mateo, California
37	Brian Hazelgren	DB	5-11	188	Fr.	Murray, Utah
	Mark Haugo	QB	6-3	190	Fr.	Minneapolis, Minnesota
70	Jim Herrmann	DE	6-6	204	Fr.	Hartland, Wisconsin
46	Tom Holmoe*	DB	6-3	182	So.	La Cresenta, California
42	Tom Hopkins (redshirt)	LB	6-2	210	So.	El Granada, California
92	Gordon Hudson	TE	6-2½	208	Fr.	Salt Lake City, Utah
	Blake Jensen	DB	5-11½	180	So.	Provo, Utah
22	Mike Jensen	DB	6-1	170	So.	Provo, Utah
16	Lee Johnson	K	6-1	183	Fr.	Houston, Texas
32	Homer Jones*	TB	5-10	198	Sr.	Honolulu, Hawaii
24	Jimmy Jones (redshirt)	TB	6-1	200	So.	Blanding, Utah
87	Lloyd Jones**	WR	6-4	187	Sr.	Pomona, California
66	Doug Kellermeyer (redshirt)	DT	6-1	240	Fr.	Scottsdale, Arizona
11	Gym Kimball	QB	6-2	180	Fr.	Salt Lake City, Utah
7	Eric Krzmarzick (redshirt)	QB	6-5	181	So.	Fallbrook, California
45	Mike Lacey*	TE	6-4	222	Jr.	Rancho Cordova, California
36	Eric Lane*	TB	6-0	195	Sr.	Hayward, California
67	Ray Linford**	OT	6-3	225	Sr.	Salt Lake City, Utah
27	John Mannion (redshirt)	DB	6-2	174	Jr.	Las Vegas, Nevada
69	Walt Manwill*	OT	6-2½	250	Jr.	Boise, Idaho
52	Trevor Matich*	C	6-4	217	So.	Sacramento, California
95	Ty Mattingly	DE	6-4	234	Fr.	Tucson, Arizona
	Keith McCullough	OG	6-2	220	Fr.	Downey, California
	Jim McDade	LB	6-1½	205	Fr.	Modesto, California
9	Jim McMahon**	QB	6-1	182	Jr.	Roy, Utah
1	Mike Mees* (redshirt)	LB	6-2	202	Jr.	Cody, Wyoming
91	David Mills	TE	6-1½	204	Fr.	Sandy, Utah
77	Mike Morgan*	DE	6-4	240	So.	Salt Lake City, Utah
83	Barry Oates	DE	6-4	235	So.	Albany, Georgia
50	Bart Oates	OT	6-4	240	So.	Albany, Georgia
35	Mike O'Neil	LB	6-1	212	So.	Hacienda Heights, California
55	Corey Pace	C	6-2	230	Jr.	Northridge, California
29	Scott Pettis	TB	5-9	185	So.	Stockton, California
20	Scott Phillips***	TB	6-2	193	Sr.	Springville, Utah
86	Dan Plater**	WR	6-2	188	Jr.	Reno, Nevada
5	Bob Prested**	DB	6-0	180	Sr.	Glendale, California
49	John Ramage*	LB	5-10	200	Jr.	Orem, Utah
26	Corey Rasmussen	DB	6-0½	180	Fr.	Salt Lake City, Utah
41	Glen Redd**	LB	6-2	229	Sr.	Ogden, Utah
64	Andy Reid*	OT	6-3	233	Sr.	Los Angeles, California
	Scott Robinson	OT	6-6	229	Fr.	Palo Alto, California
74	Steve Rogers#	OT	6-5	245	Jr.	Escondido, California
38	Ed St. Pierre**	LB	6-0	195	Sr.	Downey, California
43	Bill Schoepflin**	DB	5-10	175	Sr.	Arvada, Colorado
47	Todd Shell	LB	6-5	182	Fr.	Mesa, Arizona
23	Via Sikahema	TB	5-8	180	Fr.	Mesa, Arizona
71	Brad Smith	DT	6-4	241	Fr.	Tracy, California
58	Vince Stroth	OG	6-4	231	So.	San Jose, California
18	Ryan Tibbitts	WR	6-2	180	Sr.	Rexburg, Idaho
76	Glen Titensor*#	DE	6-4	244	Sr.	Westminster, California
53	Jeff Wadsworth	LB	6-4	188	Fr.	Salt Lake City, Utah
14	Kevin Walker	DB	5-10	190	So.	Salt Lake City, Utah
59	Kyle Whittingham**	LB	6-0	220	Jr.	Provo, Utah
17	Rob Wilson**	DB	6-0	180	Sr.	Tempe, Arizona
	Steve Young	QB	6-0½	190	Fr.	Riverside, Connecticut

*Letters   #Transfers

1980 SMU ROSTER

No.	Name	Pos.	Ht.	Wt.	Class-Exp	Hometown — High School
24	Abbe Abernathy	RB	5-10	160	Frosh	Archer City
39	Kevin Adams	LB	6-1	210	Soph-Sq	Houston (Stratton)
60	Paul Albert	OG	6-1	240	Soph-1L	Bellville
26	Dwayne Anderson	CB	6-1	175	Frosh	St. Louis, Mo. (Roosevelt)
6	Henry Andrade	WR	5-11	160	Frosh	Sacramento, Ca. (Johnson)
75	Harvey Armstrong	DT	6-2	255	Jr-2L	Houston (Kashmere)
52	Robert Barnes	OG	6-4	255	Sr-2L	Corpus Christi (King)
65	Joe Beard	OG	6-3	225	Soph-1L	Waco (Richfield)
	Peter Beath	DT	6-3	220	Soph	Dallas (Greenhill)
36	Clarence Bennett	LB	6-1	233	Sr-1L	Groveton
7	Mitchell Bennett	WR	5-10	175	Soph-Sq	Bonham
25	Dick Blaylock	CB	5-10	170	Sr-2L	Dallas (St. Marks)
37	Todd Boales	DE	6-2	180	Frosh	Uvalde
87	Rickey Bolden	TE	6-5	237	Frosh	Dallas (Hillcrest)
57	Aaron Boulton	OT	6-4	245	Frosh	Dallas (Wilson)
27	Charles Bruton	CB	5-11	192	Sr-3L	Nacogdoches
95	Grady Burnette	NG	6-3	243	Frosh	Georgetown
74	Michael Carter	NG	6-2	265	Soph-1L	Dallas (Thomas Jefferson)
20	Russell Carter	3	6-3	180	Frosh	Philadelphia, Pa. (Lower Merion)
98	Kevin Chaney	DT	6-2	225	Soph-1L	Conroe
42	Michael Charles	RB	6-0	205	Soph-1L	Houston (Kashmere)
14	Jeff Courtwright	QB	5-10	185	Soph-Sq	Dallas (Lake Highlands)
19	Eric Dickerson	RB	6-3	205	Soph-1L	Sealy
91	Roy Douglas	DE	6-3	215	Sr-1L	Nacogdoches
28	Charles Drayton	FB	5-10	205	Soph-Sq	Indian Town, Fla.
31	David Dykhuizen	FB	6-1	220	Sr-1L	Spring (Klein)
99	Eric Ferguson	DE	6-3	245	Jr-2L	Houston (Kashmere)
17	Mike Fisher	QB	6-4	205	Soph-Sq	Waco (Richfield)
10	Mike Ford	QB	6-3	220	Jr-2L	Mesquite
86	Clement Fox	TB	6-2	220	Sr-1L	Shreveport, La.
83	Byron Frierson	DE	6-5	230	Frosh	Indianapolis, Ind. (Manual)
1	Eddie Garcia	K	5-9	175	Jr-2L	Dallas (Wilson)
9	Mark Gibson	S-WR	6-1	195	Sr-3L	Duncanville
94	Scott Gibson	NG	6-3	230	Soph-1L	Duncanville
41	Tony Giuliani	NG	6-0	249	Frosh	Columbus, Ohio (Westerville)
30	Standley Godine	DB	6-1	185	Soph-Sq	Houston (Kashmere)
	Tony Good	OLB	5-11	190	Soph-Sq	Northfield, Ill.
53	Forrest Gregg, Jr.	C	6-2	215	Frosh	Parma, Ohio (Padua)
3	Jeff Harrall	K	6-1	173	Frosh	Houston
77	Perry Hartnett	OG	6-8	260	Jr-2L	Galveston (Ball)
46	Wes Hopkins	S	5-11	189	Soph-1L	Birmingham, Ala.
80	Byron Hunt	DE	6-5	240	Sr-3L	Longview (White Oak)
61	Chris Jackson	OG	6-2	220	Frosh	Houston (Stratford)
32	Craig James	RB	6-1	210	Soph-1L	Houston (Stratford)
45	Lee Jeans	WR	6-1	200	Sr-Sq	Santa Fe (Alta Loma)
62	Kevin Jennings	OG	6-3	240	Soph-Sq	Plano
13	John Joplin	WR	5-8	156	Soph-Sq	Garland
71	Mike Jusko	OT	6-6	267	Sr-3L	Granada Hills, Calif.
7	Eric Keiter	P	6-3	500	Jr-Tr	Kansas City (Bishop Ward)
68	Tab Keener	OT	6-2	245	Soph-Sq	Canyon
51	James Lorfing	OT	6-6	245	Frosh	Channelview
44	Efrem Lynch	FB	6-1	230	Soph-Sq	Dallas (Roosevelt)
79	David Marshall	DT	6-5	250	Sr-3L	Monroe, Ohio
67	Mike Mason	OG	6-4	245	Sr-2L	Palestine
55	Gordon McAdams	C	6-0	220	Jr-2L	Denton
64	Harvey McAtee	NG	5-11	200	Sr-Sq	Houston (Northbrook)
11	Lance McIlhenny	QB	5-10	180	Frosh	Dallas (Highland Park)
40	Lott McIlhenny	TE	6-2	230	Soph-1L	Dallas (Highland Park)
	Dan McVicker	DE	6-1	222	Soph-Tr	Irving (Air Force Academy)
20	James Mobley	S	6-0	185	Jr-1L	Tyler
92	Eric Moore	LB	5-11	213	Soph-Sq	Waxahachie
90	Jared Moore	DE	6-0	215	Jr-2L	Denison
18	Todd Moore	DE	5-11	185	Soph-Sq	Dallas (Cistercian)
33	Gary Moten	LB	6-2	195	Soph-Sq	Shreveport, La.
78	Richard Neely	DT	6-5	238	Soph-Sq	Dallas (Highland Park)
8	Fred Nichols	CB	5-11	180	Frosh	Killeen
22	Edward O'Brien	RB	6-0	185	Soph-Sq	Pasadena (Dobie)
72	Brian O'Meara	OT	6-6	250	Soph-Sq	Cleveland, Ohio
15	Matt Orefice	K	6-3	175	Frosh	New Canaan, Conn.
50	Lance Pederson	C	6-1	240	Sr-3L	Austin (Anderson)
35	Mathis Perkins	CB	5-10	175	Jr-Sq	Dallas (South Oak Cliff)
5	Reginald Phillips	CB	5-9	170	Frosh	Houston (Yates)
85	David Randle	TE	6-4	230	Frosh	Dallas (White)
70	Mike Randle	C	6-3	236	Jr-1L	Dallas (White)
88	Norm Revis	TE	6-3	225	Soph	Diamond Bar, Ca. (Bishop Amat)
54	Ken Roberts	OG	6-2	245	Frosh	San Antonio (Wheatley)
73	Rickey Schulte	OT	6-2	235	Jr-Sq	Victoria
34	John Simmons	CB	5-11	188	Sr-3L	Little Rock (Parkview)
97	Victor Simon	DE	6-2	210	Jr-Tr	Houston (Smiley)
81	Anthony Smith	WR	5-11	186	Sr-3L	Houston (Kashmere)
23	Blane Smith	S	6-0	191	Soph-1L	Houston (Yates)
89	Gary Smith	SE	6-0	183	Jr-2L	Houston (Kashmere)
76	Lee Spivey	OT	6-2	270	Sr-2L	Houston (Kashmere)
63	Steve Staniland	OG	6-5	275	Jr-Tr	Oxnard, Calif.
48	Quinten Stephens	FB	5-11	195	Frosh	Garland
69	David Temples	OT	6-1	236	Soph-Sq	Mt. Pleasant
66	Waldo Theus	LB	5-11	217	Jr-1L	Little Rock (Parkview)
56	Mark Thompson	C	6-1	230	Soph-Sq	Arvada, Colo. (West)
43	Rick Touton	NG	6-0	215	Frosh	Robinson
59	Mike Washburn	DL	6-5	225	Frosh	Amarillo (Tascosa)
93	Russell Washington	DE	6-0	201	Soph-1L	Fort Worth (Wyatt)
98	Mitch Willis	DT	6-6	230	Frosh	Arlington (Lamar)
49	Sterling Wilson	CB	5-9	189	Soph-Sq	Austin (Anderson)
4	Jeff Wood	K	5-10	177	Frosh	Arlington
96	Steve Wright	DT	6-2	205	Soph-Sq	Lubbock (Estacado)

BRIGHAM YOUNG UNIVERSITY
The Cougars

 Brad Anae, 93

 Robert Anae, 57

 Rob Andersen, 80

 David Aupiu, 44

 Neil Balhom, 89

 Mark Brady, 12

 Steve Brady, 13

 Matt Braga, 19

 Clay Brown, 85

 Royce Bybee, 10

 Pat Cabulagan, 28

 Steve Carlsen, 5

 Calvin Close, 63

 Scott Collie, 3

 Bill Davis, 88

 Chuck Ehin, 78

 Lloyd Eldredge, 56

 Nick Eyre, 72

 Wayne Faalafua, 75

 Brandon Flint, 99

 Dave Francis, 8

 Kurt Gunther, 2

 Larry Hamilton

 Waymon Hamilton

| Bruce Hansen, 34 | Brad Hardisty, 84 | Mark Haugo | Adam Haysbert | Brian Hazelgren, 37 | Jim Herrmann, 70 |

| Tom Holmoe, 46 | Tom Hopkins, 42 | Gordon Hudson, 92 | Blake Jensen | Mike Jensen, 22 | Lee Johnson, 16 |

| Homer Jones, 32 | Jimmy Jones, 24 | | | Lloyd Jones, 87 | Doug Kellermeyer, 6 |

| Eric Krzmarzick, 7 | Mike Lacey, 45 | Eric Lane, 36 | Ray Linford, 67 | Walt Manwill, 69 | Trevor Matich, 52 |

| Ty Mattingly, 95 | Keith McCullough | Jim McDade | Jim McMahon, 9 | Mike Mees, 1 | David Mills, 91 |

Mike Morgan, 77

Barry Oates, 83

Bart Oates, 50

Mike O'Neil, 35

Scott Pettis, 29

Cory Pace, 5

Scott Phillips, 20

Dan Plater, 86

Bob Prested, 5

John Ramage, 49

Korey Rasmussen, 26

Glen Redd, 41

Andy Reid, 64

Scott Robinson

Steve Rogers, 74

Ed St. Pierre, 38

Bill Schoepflin, 43

Todd Shell, 47

Vai Sikahema, 23

Brad Smith, 71

Vince Stroth, 58

Ryan Tibbitts, 18

Glen Titensor, 76

Jeff Wadsworth, 53

Kevin Walker, 14

Kyle Whittingham, 59

Rob Wilson, 17

Steve Young

National Collegiate Athletic Association
OFFICIAL SCORING SUMMARY

SOUTHERN METHODIST   vs.   BRIGHAM YOUNG

Visitors   Home   50,200

Date Friday, Dec. 19, 1980   Site San Diego, California   Attendance ~~50,214~~

THIRD ANNUAL HOLIDAY BOWL

Score by Quarters	1	2	3	4	Final
SOUTHERN METHODIST	19	10	9	7	43
BRIGHAM YOUNG	7	6	6	27	46

						SMU	BYU
MU	1	2:03	Dickerson, 15 run (Garcia kick)	(4/53)		7	0
MU	1	5:00	James, 45 run (Garcia kick)	(4/54)		14	0
MU	1	8:04	Safety, centered out of end zone			16	0
MU	1	10:39	FG, Garcia 42	(8/38)		19	0
YU	1	12:26	Brown, 64 pass from McMahon (Gunther kick)	(4/80)		19	7
MU	2	3:04	James, 3 pass from McIlhenny (Garcia kick)	(8/54)		26	7
MU	2	8:13	FG, Garcia 44	(6/29)		29	7
YU	2	13:50	Sikahema, 83 punt return (pass failed)			29	13
MU	3	5:23	Dickerson, 1 run (pass failed)	(12/75)		35	13
YU	3	8:20	Brown, 13 pass from McMahon (pass failed)	(10/80)		35	19
MU	3	13:45	FG, Garcia 42	(12/37)		38	19
YU	4	10:53	Phillips, 1 run (pass failed)	(17/90)		38	25
MU	4	11:03	James, 42 run (Garcia kick)	(1/42)		45	25
YU	4	12:27	Braga, 15 pass from McMahon (pass failed)	(7/72)		45	31
YU	4	13:02	Phillips, 1 run (pass to Phillips)	(4/50)		45	39
YU	4	15:00	Brown, 41 pass from McMahon (Gunther kick)	(3/41)		45	46

Most Valuable Player: Offense – SMU Craig James & BYU Jim McMahon
Defense – SMU Michael Carter

Attendance: 50,214 paid

Time of Game: Kickoff 6:11   End of Game 9:41   Total Elapsed Time 3:30

Officials (BIG 8 CONFERENCE) Referee John McClintock, Umpire Bob Kleaves, Linesman

Charles Weems, Line Judge Frank Gaines, Field Judge Tom Fincher, Back Judge Virgil Downing

Temperature 64   Wind 2 mph Westerly   Weather overcast

Sample scoring descriptions:
Winsockie—Smith 6 run (Jones run) 8:56
Tech—Jones 22 pass from Brown (Williams kick) 4:33
Winsockie—Smith 3 run (kick failed) 13:08
Tech—FG Jones, 23, 2:12
Winsockie—Safety, Smith tackled Jones in endzone, 5th
Tech—Jones 13 run (Jones pass from Brown) 1:57

National Collegiate Athletic Association
FINAL INDIVIDUAL STATISTICS

SOUTHERN METHODIST — Visitors

Rushing

Rushing	Att.	Gain	Lost	Net	TD	Long
MCILHENNY	14	65	19	46	0	18
JAMES	23	225	0	225	2	45
DICKERSON	23	120	10	110	2	28
CHARLES	5	12	0	12	0	4
DYKHUIZEN	1	0	0	0	0	0
Totals	66	422	29	393	4	45

Passing

Passing	Att.-Comp.-Int.	Yards	TD	Long
MCILHENNY	11-6-0	53	1	20
Totals	11-6-0	53	1	20

Pass Receiving

Pass Receiving	No.	Yards	TD	Long
DICKERSON	1	5	0	5
M. BENNETT	1	20	0	20
JAMES	2	13	1	10
A. SMITH	1	10	0	10
FOX	1	5	0	5
Totals	6	53	1	20

Punting

Punting	No.	Yds.	Avg.	Long
KAIPES	4	155	38.8	51
Totals				

Field Goals

Field Goals	Att.	Made	Long
GARCIA	3	3	44
Totals	3	3	44

All Returns

All Returns	Punts No.	Punts Yds.	Kickoffs No.	Kickoffs Yds.	Intercepted No.	Intercepted Yds.
BLAYLOCK	0	0	3	75	0	0
SIMMONS	1	0	1	10	0	0
BRUTON					1	0
Totals	1	0	4	85	1	0

BRIGHAM YOUNG — Home Team

Rushing

Rushing	Att.	Gain	Lost	Net	TD	Long
S. PHILLIPS	8	24	6	18	2	9
McMAHON	10	36	36	0	0	20
LANE	4	1	3	-2	0	1
PETTIS	1	5	0	5	0	5
CENTER PASS	1	0	-23	-23	0	0
Totals	24	66	68	-2	2	20

Passing

Passing	Att.-Comp.-Int.	Yards	TD	Long
McMAHON	49-32-1	446	4	64
Totals	49-32-1	446	4	64

Pass Receiving

Pass Receiving	No.	Yards	TD	Long
S. PHILLIPS	10	81	0	14
C. BROWN	5	155	3	64
BRAGA	5	77	1	22
DAVIS	4	75	0	40
PLATER	2	9	0	6
L. JONES	3	31	0	14
LANE	2	9	0	8
PETTIS	1	9	0	9
TOTAL	32	446	4	64

Punting

Punting	No.	Yds.	Avg.	Long
C. BROWN	5	163	32.6	35
Totals	5	163	32.6	35

Field Goals

Field Goals	Att.	Made	Long
NONE			
Totals			

All Returns

All Returns	Punts No.	Punts Yds.	Kickoffs No.	Kickoffs Yds.	Intercepted No.	Intercepted Yds.
SIKAHEMA	2	87	3	55	0	0
SCHOEPFLIN	1	11	0	0	0	0
HANSEN	0	0	1	10	0	0
Totals	3	98	4	65	0	0

National Collegiate Athletic Association
FINAL TEAM STATISTICS

	SOUTHERN METHODIST	BRIGHAM YOUNG
First Downs	25	23
Rushing	18	2
Passing	4	21
Penalty	3	0
Rushing Attempts	66	24
Yards Rushing	422	66
Yards Lost Rushing	29	68
Net Yards Rushing	393	-2
Net Yards Passing	53	446
Passes Attempted	11	49
Passes Completed	6	32
Had Intercepted	0	1
Total Offensive Plays	77	73
Total Net Yards	446	444
Average Gain Per Play	5.8	6.1
Fumbles: Number—Lost	2–0	2–0
Penalties: Number—Yards	7–65	8–80
Interceptions: Number—Yards	1–0	0–0
Number of Punts—Yards	4–155	5–163
Average Per Punt	38.8	32.6
Punt Returns: Number—Yards	1–0	3–98
Kickoff Returns: Number—Yards	4–85	4–65

BYU won coin toss & elected to receive. SMU will defend east goal.

Garcia kicks off to Sikahema in end zone for touchback.

BYU 15:00
1-10 C-20 Phillips up middle for 8 to 28 (Moten)
2- 2 C-28 McMahon pass, incomplete Cartef deflects
3- 2 C-28 Delay of game BYU 5 yards
3- 7 C-23 McMahon pass intended for C.Brown, incomplete
4- 7 C-23 C.Brown punts to Blaylock, fair catch at M-48 (29 punt)

   SMU 14:06
   1-10 M-48 McIlhenny around right end for 12 to C-40 (Redd)   FIRST DOWN RUSH
   1-10 C-40 James at left tackle for 3 to 37 (Anne)
   2- 7 C-37 James around right end for 22 to 15 (Prestad, Titensor)   FIRST DOWN RUSH
   1-10 C-15 Dickerson around left end for 15 yard t TD
4 plays 52 yards Elapsed Time 2:03 Garcia PAT good   SMU 7 BYU 0

Garcia kicks off to Sikahema in end zone for touchback

BYU 12:57
1-10 C-20 McMahon, back to pass, runs to 2 to 22 (Carter, Armstrong)
2- 8 C-22 McMahon pass intended for B.Davis, incomplete (Moten)
3- 8 C-22 McMahon pass intended for L.Jones, incomplete (Bruton)
4- 8 C-22 C.Brown punts to Simmons, fumbles recovers at M-46 (32 punt)

   SMU 11:58
   1-10 M-46 James up middle for 3 to 49 (Redd)
   2- 7 M-49 McIlhenny around left end for 4 to C-47 (Redd, Whittingham)
   3- 3 C-47 James at left tackle for 2 to 45 (Ehin)
   4- 1 C-45 James, on fake punt, runs for 45 yard TD
4 plays 54 yards Elapsed Time 5:00 Garcia PAT good   SMU 14 BYU 0

Garcia kicks off to end zone for touchback

BYU 10:00
1-10 C-20 Phillips at left end for loss of 5 to 15 (Bennett)
2-15 C-15 Phillips up middle for 9 to 24 (Washington)
3- 6 C-24 McMDahon, back to pass, runs to 23 for loss of 1 (Armstrong)
4- 7 C-23 C.Brown back to punt, snap over punters head to end zone for safety
Elapsed Time 6:56   SMU 16   BYU 0

Johnson kicks off from 20 to Simmons at 27, returns to 37 for 10 (Walker)
SMU 7:58
1-10 M-37 Dickerson at right end for 7 to 44 (Schletflin)
2- 3 M-44 Dickerson up middle for 4 to 48 ((St. Pierre, Prestad)   FIRST DOWN RUSH
1-10 M-48 Dickerson up middle for 11 to C-41 (Holome)   FDLRT DOWN RUSH
1-10 C-41 James up middle for 2 to 39 (Whittingham)
2- 8 C-39 James at right end for 9 to 30 (Prestad Anne)   FIRST DOWN RUSH
1-10 C-30 Dickerson at right tackle for 7 to 23 (St. Peirer, Shoelplin)
2- 3 C-23 Dickerson at left tackle for loss of 2 to 25 (Anne, Whittingham)
3- 5 C-25 McIlhenny pass intended for A.Smith, incomplete (Schoelplin)
4- 5 C-25 Garcia kicks 42 yard field goal
8 plays 38 yards   Elapsed Time 10:39   SMU 19   BYU 0

Garcia kicks off out of bounds 5 yard penalty
Garcia kicks off from 35 out of bounds 5 yard penalty
Garcia kicks off to Sikahema at 3, returns to 20 (Thas)

BYU 4:16
1-10 C-20 Phillips at right guard for 3 to 23 (Hunt)
2- 7 C-23 McMahon pass complete to Phillips for 8 to 31 (Mobley, Moten)   FIRST DOWN PASS
1-10 C-31 McMahon pass complete to Phillips for 5 to 36 (Bennett)
2- 5 C-36 McMahon pass complete to C.Brown for 64 yard TD   FIRST DOWN PASS
4 plays 80 yards   Elapsed Time 12:26 Gunther PAT good   SMU 19 BYU 7

Johnson kicks off to Simmons in end zone for touchback
   SMU 2:34
   1-10 M-20 James around right end for 14 to 34 (Prestedd)   FIRST DOWN RUSH
   1-10 M-34 James up middle for 1 to 35 (Whittingham)
   2- 9 M-35 McIlhenny around left end for 2 to 37 (Redd)
   3- 7 M-37 McIlhenny on draw up middle for 4 to 41 (Anne)
   4- 3 M-41 Kaifes punts to Sikahema at 3, fumbles, recovers at 12 (51 punt)
BYU 0:D16
1-10 C-12 Phillips up middle for 2 to 14 (Hunt, Moten)

   END OF FIRST QUARTER 6:54 PM   SMU 19 BYU 7

3RD DOWN CON
BYU   SMU
0/3   1/3

National Collegiate Athletic Association
QUICKIE STATISTICS

First Quarter (circled)   Half   Third Quarter   Final

(Circle One)

TEAM

	SOUTHERN METHODIST Visitors	BRIGHAM YOUNG Home Team
Score	19	7
First Downs	8	2
Rushes—Yardage (Net)	165	-5
Passing Yardage (Net)	0	77
*Return Yardage (Net)	0	4
Passes—Att.-Comp.-Int.	1 - 0 - 0	7 - 3 - 0
Total Offense—Yards	165	72
Punts (Number-Average)	1 - 51 - 51.0	2 - 61 - 30.5
Fumbles—Lost	1 - 0	1 - 0
Penalties—Yards	2 - 10	1 - 5

*Return of Punts, Intercepted Passes and Fumbles (not Kickoffs).

INDIVIDUAL LEADERS

SOUTHERN METHODIST — Visitors

Rushing	Att.	Net Yards	TD	Long
JAMES	9	101	1	45
DICKERSON	6	42	1	15

Passing	Att.-Comp.-Int.	Yds.	TD
McILHENNY	1 - 0 - 0	0	0

Pass Receiving	No.	Yards	TD	Long
NONE				

Punting	No.	Avg.	Long
KAIFES	1	51.0	51

BRIGHAM YOUNG — Home Team

Rushing	Att.	Net Yards	TD	Long
S. PHILLIPS	6	16	0	8
McMAHON	1	2	0	2

Passing	Att.-Comp.-Int.	Yds.	TD
McMAHON	7 - 3 - 0	77	1

Pass Receiving	No.	Yards	TD	Long
S. PHILLIPS	2	13	0	13
C. BROWN	1	64	1	64

Punting	No.	Avg.	Long
C. BROWN	2	30.5	32

BYU
2- 8 C-14 McMahon pass intended for Plater, intercepted by Bruton at M-46 (Plater)

    SMU 15:00
    1-10 M-46 Dickerson up middle 6 to C-48 (Anae, Redd)
    2- 4 C-48 Charles up middle for 1 to 47 (1Whittingham)
    3-3 C-47 McIlhenny pass complete to Dickerson for 5 to 42 (Solom) roughing passer (Whitting   FIRST DOWN PASS
               15 yards
    1-10 C-27 McIlhenny pass complete to Bennett for 20 to 7 (Schoeflin)   FIRST DOWN PENALTY
               Unsportsmanlike conduct (Schoeflin)   FIRST DOWN PENALTY
    1- G C- 4 2 James at right guard for 3 to 1 (Whittingham)
    2- G C- 1 Dickerson at right end for loss of 2 to 3 (Anae, St.Peirre)
    3- G C- 3 McIlhenny pass complete to James for 3 yard TD   FIRST DOWN PASS
    8 plays 54 yards Elapsed Time 3:04 Garcia PAT good SMU 28 BYU 7
Garcia kicks off to Sikahema at goal line, returns to 16 (Simon)
BYU 11:51
1-10 C-16 McMahon, back to pass, runs to 12 for loss of 4 (Carter)
2-14 C-12 McMahon pass intended for Lane, incomplete (B.Smith)
3-14 C-12 McMahon pass complete to Braga for 19 to 31 (Carter)   FIRST DOWN PASS
1-10 C-31 McMahon pass intended for Phillips incomplete (M.Carter deflected)
2-10 C-31 McMahon fumbles snap, recovers at 30 for loss of 1 (Chaney)
3-11 C-30 McMahon sacked by B.Smith for loss of 9 to 21
4-20 C-21 C.Brown punts to Simmons, fair catch at M-44 (35 punt)

    SMU 10:00
    1-10 M-44 Dickerson at right guard for no gain (1Whittingham, Titensor)
    2-10 M-44 McIlhenny pass intended for G.Smith, incomplete NO PLAY PASS INTERFERENCE
               12 yard penalty   FIRST DOWN PENALTY
    1-10 C-44 Dickerson up middle for 3 to 41 (St.Peirre, Titensor)
    2- 7 C-41 McIlhenny around left end for 13 to 28 (Whittingham)   FIRST DOWN RUSH
    1-10 C-28 Charles up middle for 3 to 25 (Whittingham)
    2- 7 C-25 Dickerson at right end for loss of 2 to 27 (Titensor)
    3- 9 C-27 McIlhenny pass intended for James, incomplete
    4- 9 C-27 Garcia kicks 44 yard field goal
    6 plays 29 yards SMU 29 BYU 7   Elapsed Time 8:13
Garcia kicks off to Sikahema at goal line, returns to 22 (Phillips)
BYU 6:42
1-10 C-22 McMahon pass complete to Brage for 22 to 44 (F.Carter)   FIRST DOWN PASS
1-10 C-44 McMahon pass complete to B.Davis for 11 to M-45 (Blaylock)   FIRST DOWN PASS
1-10 M-45 McMahon sacked by Armstrong for loss of 6 to C-49
2-16 C-49 Lane up middle for loss of 3 to 46 (M.Carter, Armstrong)
3-19 C-46 McMahon pass intended for Braga incomplete (Blaylock)
4-19 C-46 C.Brown punts to 29 (24) interference on Hermann, 14 yards
    SMU 4:24   19 (35 punt)
    1-10 M-34 James at right end for 11 to 45 (Redd)   FIRST DOWN RUSH
    1-10 M-45 McIlhenny runs right end for no gain (Anae)
    2-10 M-45 Charles up middle for 1 to 46 (Whittingham)
    3- 9 M-46 McIlhenny pass complete to Fox for 8 to C-46 NO PLAY PASS INTERFERENCE BYU
               3 yard penalty   FIRST DOWN PENALTY
    1-10 M-49 McIlhenny pass intended for Fox, incomplete NO PLAY HOLDING SMU
    1-25 M-34 Dickerson at left end for loss of 3 to 31 (Anae)
    2-28 M-31 Dickerson at right tackle for 8 to 39 (Prested)
    3-20 M-39 Dickerson up middle for 3 to 42 (Whittingham, Titensor)
    4-17 M-42 Kaifes punts to Sikahema at 17, returns for 83 yard TD (41 punt)
Schoepflin attempts pass to Carlsen for 2 point attempt- no good SMU 29 BYU 13

Johnson kicks off to Blaylock at goal line, returns to 21 (Jensen) Clipping BYU 15 yards
    SMU 1:04
    1-10 M-36 McIlhenny pass intended for Dickerson, incomplete (Schoepflin)
    2-10 M-36 McIlhenny pass complete to James for 10 to 46 (Brady)   FIRST DOWN PASS
    1-10 M-46 James up middle for 6 to C-48 (Ehin)
    2- 4 C-48 McIlhenny pass intended for James, incomplete
    3- 4 C-48 McIlhenny sacked by Ehin for loss of 6 to M-46
    4-10 SM-46 Kaifes punts, ball downed at C-26 (28 punt)
BYU 00:06
1-10 C-26 McMahon pass intended for Brage, incomplete (Simmons)

    END OF FIRST HALF 7:44 PM SMU 29 BYU 13

3RD Down Brn

BYU   SMU
1/3   2/5

National Collegiate Athletic Association
QUICKIE STATISTICS

First Quarter   (Half)   Third Quarter   Final

(Circle One)

TEAM

	SOUTHERN METHODIST Visitors	BRIGHAM YOUNG Home Team
Score	29	13
First Downs	16	5
Rushes—Yardage (Net)	210	-28
Passing Yardage (Net)	38	129
*Return Yardage (Net)	0	87
Passes—Att.-Comp.-Int.	8-4-0	15-6-1
Total Offense—Yards	248	101
Punts (Number-Average)	3-120-40.0	4-131-32.8
Fumbles—Lost	1-0	2-0
Penalties—Yards	3-25	7-68

*Return of Punts, Intercepted Passes and Fumbles (not Kickoffs).

INDIVIDUAL LEADERS

SOUTHERN METHODIST — Visitors

Rushing	Att.	Net Yards	TD	Long
JAMES	12	121	1	45
DICKERSON	14	55	1	15

Passing	Att.-Comp.-Int.	Yds.	TD
McILHENNY	8-4-0	38	1

Pass Receiving	No.	Yards	TD	Long
M. BENNETT	1	20	0	20
JAMES	2	13	1	10

Punting	No.	Avg.	Long
KAIFES	3	40.0	51

BRIGHAM YOUNG — Home Team

Rushing	Att.	Net Yards	TD	Long
S. PHILLIPS	6	16	0	9
McMAHON	5	-18	0	2

Passing	Att.-Comp.-Int.	Yds	TD
McMAHON	15-6-1	129	1

Pass Receiving	No.	Yards	TD	Long
C. BROWN	1	64	1	64
BRAGA	2	41	0	22
S. PHILLIPS	2	13	0	8

Punting	No.	Avg.	Long
C. BROWN	4	32.8	35

Johnson kicks off to Blaylock at 4, returns to 25 (Wilson)

SMU 14:55

1-10 M-25	James up middle for 2 to 27 (Whittingham)	
2- 8 M-27	McIlhenny at right end for 3 to 30 (St. Pierre)	
3- 5 M-30	James around left end for 10 to 40 (St. Pierre)	FIRST DOWN RUSH
1-10 M-40	James around right end for 2 to 42 (St.Pierre, Prested)	
2- 8 M-42	Charles up middle for 3 to 45 (Whittingham)	
3- 5 M-45	Dickerson around left end for 28 to C-27 (Brady)	FIRST DOWN RUSH
1-10 C-27	McIlhenny around right end for 6 to 21 (Holme)	
2- 4 C-21	Dickerson up middle for 4 to 17 (Redd, Whittingham)	FIRST DOWN RUSH
1-10 C-17	Dickerson up middle for 4 to 13 (Redd, Prested)	
2- 6 C-13	James at right tackle for 10 to 3 (Holme, Redd)	FIRST DOWN RUSH
1- G C- 3	James up middle for 2 to 1 (Whittingham, Morgan)	
2- G C- 1	Dickerson up middle for 1 yard TD	

12 plays 75 yards Elapsed Time 5:23 McIlhenny pass intended for James no good PAT
SMU 35   BYU 13

Garcia kicks off to Sikahema in end zone for touchback

BYU 9:37

1-10 C-20	McMahon pass complete to Plater for 6 to 26	
2- 4 C-26	McMahon pass complete to Phillips for 12 to 38 (B.Hunt)	FIRST DOWN PASS
1-10 C-38	McMahon pass complete to Phillips for 5 to 43 (M.Carter)	
2- 5 C-43	McMahon pass complete to Phillips for 7 to 50 (Molten)	FIRST DOWN PASS
1-10 50	McMahon, back to pass, runs to 30 for 20 (Bruton)	FIRST DOWN RUSH
1-10 M-30	Lane up middle for 1 to 29 (Armstrong)	
2- 9 M-29	McMahon pass complete to Phillips for 11 to 18	FIRST DOWN PASS
1-10 M-18	McMahon pass intended for Braga, incomplete (Chaney)	
2-10 M-18	Pettis around left end for 5 to 13 (Bruton)	
3- 5 M-13	McMahon pass complete to C.Brown for 13 yard TD	FIRST DOWN PASS

10 plays 80 yards Elapsed Time 8:20 McMahon pass intended for Slater PAT no good
SMU 35   BYU 19

Johnson kicks off to Blaylock at 5, returns to 38 (Holmoe, Schoepflin)

SMU 6:32

1-10 M-38	Charles up middle for 4 to 42 (Morgan)	
2- 6 M-42	James around right end for 15 to C-43 (Redd)	FIRST DOWN RUSH
1-10 C-43	Dickerson up middle for 5 to 38 (Redd, Schoepflin)	
2- 5 C-38	Dickerson at right tackle for 4 to 34 (Prested)	
3- 1 C-34	Illegal Procedure SMU 5 yards	
3- 6 C-39	McIlhenny pass complete to A.Smith for 10 to 29 (St.Pierre, Schoepflin)	FIRST DOWN
1-10 C-29	Dykhulzen up middle for no gain (Titesnor)	
2-10 C-29	McIlhenny at right end for loss of 4 to 33 (Titensor)	
3-14 C-33	McIlhenny, back to pass, runs to 15 for 18 (Redd)	FIRST DOWN RUSH
1-10 C-15	James around left end for 9 to 6 (Holmoe) Clipping SMU 6 rush for James	
1-19 C-24	Dickerson around right end for 16 to 8 (Schoepflin)	
2-11 C-16	McIlhenny pass intended for A.Smith incomplete	
3-11 C-16	McIlhenny sacked by Redd for loss of 9 to 25	
4-20 C-25	Garcia kicks 42 yard field goal	

12 plays 37 yards Elapsed Time 13:45   SMU 38   BYU 19

Garcia kicks off to Sikahema in end zone for touchback

BYU 1:15

1-10 C-20	McMahon pass complete to B.Davis for 15 to 35 (Bruton)	FIRST DOWN PASS
1-10 C-35	McMahon sacked by Armstrong for loss of 10 to 25 Personal Foul BYU 12 yards	
2-32 C-13	McMahon pass complete to B.Davis for 9 to 22 (Moten) Personal Foul Smu 15 yards	
3- 8 C-37	McMahon sacked for loss of 4 to 33 (M.Carter)	
4-12 C-33		

END OF THIRD QUARTER   SMU 38 BYU 19
8:51 PM

3RD DOWN CONV

BYU   SMU
1/1   3/4

National Collegiate Athletic Association
QUICKIE STATISTICS

First Quarter   Half   (Third Quarter)   Final

(Circle One)

TEAM

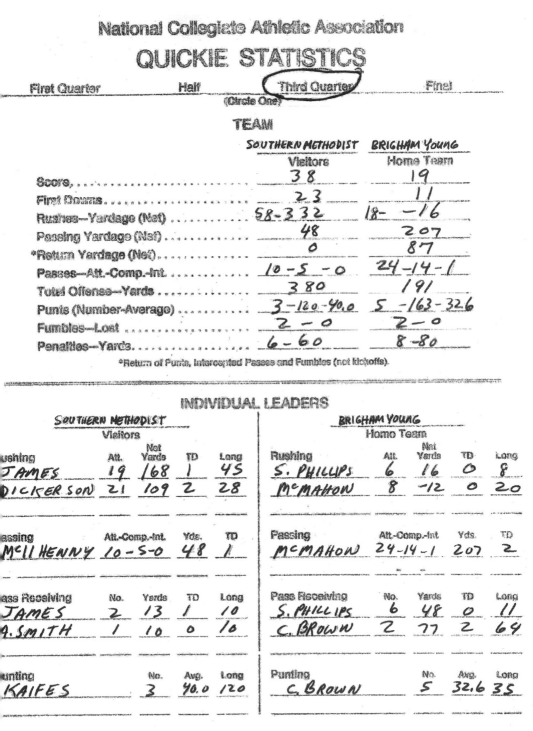

	SOUTHERN METHODIST Visitors	BRIGHAM YOUNG Home Team
Score	38	19
First Downs	23	11
Rushes—Yardage (Net)	58-332	18- -16
Passing Yardage (Net)	48	207
*Return Yardage (Net)	0	87
Passes—Att.-Comp.-Int.	10 - 5 - 0	24 -14 - 1
Total Offense—Yards	380	191
Punts (Number-Average)	3 - 120 - 40.0	5 - 163 - 32.6
Fumbles—Lost	2 - 0	2 - 0
Penalties—Yards	6 - 60	8 - 80

*Return of Punts, Intercepted Passes and Fumbles (not kickoffs).

INDIVIDUAL LEADERS

SOUTHERN METHODIST — Visitors

Rushing	Att.	Net Yards	TD	Long
JAMES	19	168	1	45
DICKERSON	21	109	2	28

Passing	Att.-Comp.-Int.	Yds.	TD
McILHENNY	10 - 5 - 0	48	1

Pass Receiving	No.	Yards	TD	Long
JAMES	2	13	1	10
A. SMITH	1	10	0	10

Punting	No.	Avg.	Long
KAIFES	3	40.0	120

BRIGHAM YOUNG — Home Team

Rushing	Att.	Net Yards	TD	Long
S. PHILLIPS	6	16	0	8
McMAHON	8	-12	0	20

Passing	Att.-Comp.-Int.	Yds.	TD
McMAHON	24 -14 - 1	207	2

Pass Receiving	No.	Yards	TD	Long
S. PHILLIPS	6	48	0	11
C. BROWN	2	77	2	64

Punting	No.	Avg.	Long
C. BROWN	5	32.6	35

BYU

4-12 C-33 C.Brown punt to M-35 (32 punt) ball downed

     SMU 14:50
     1-10 M-35 James at left guard for 8 to 43 (Holmoe, Prested)
     2- 2 M-43 James up middle for 4 to 47 (Morgan)
     1-10 M-47 McIlhenny pass complete to Fox for 5 to C-48 (Brady)   FIRST DOWN RUSH
     2- 5 C-48 James up middle for 3 to 45 (Morgan, Titensor)
     3- 2 C-45 McIlhenny at left end for no gain (Whittingham, St.Pierre)
     4- 2 C-45 Kaifes punts to Sikahema, fair catch at 10 (35 punt)

BYU 11:37
     1-10 C-10 McMahon pass complete to Plater for 3 to 13 (Moten)
     2- 7 C-13 McMahon pass complete to Braga for 11 to 24   FIRST DOWN PASS
     1-10 C-24 McMahon pass complete to Phillips for 14 to 38 (Moten) FIRST DOWN PASS
     1-10 C-38 McMahon pass complete to L.Jones for 7 to 45 (Bennett)
     2- 3 C-45 McMahon pass complete to Lane for 1 to 46 (Bruton)
     3- 2 C-46 McMahon pass intended for Braga, incomplete (heavy rush by Washington)
     4- 2 C-46 McMahon pass complete to C.Brown for 12 to M-42 (Mobley, Blaylock) FIRST DOWN PASS
     1-10 M-42 McMahon pass complete to Braga for 10 to 32 (Bruton)   FIRST DOWN PASS
     1-10 M-32 McMahon sacked by Neely for loss of 2 to 34
     2-12 M-34 McMahon pass complete to L.Jones for 14 to 20 (Bruton) FIRST DOWN PASS
     1-10 M-20 McMahon pass intended for B.Davis, incomplete
     2-10 M-20 McMahon pass complete to Phillips for 5 to 15
     3- 5 M-15 McMahon pass complete to Phillips for 4 to 11 (Bennett)
     4- 1 M-11 McMahon pass complete to L.Jones for 10 to 1 (Bruton) FIRST DOWN PASS
     1- G M- 1 Lane at right guard for no gain (Moten)
     2- G M- 1 Lane at right tackle for no gain (Bennett)
     3- G M- 1 Phillips around left end for 1 yard TD
17 plays 90 yards Elapsed Time 10:53 McMahon pass intended for Braga for PAT no good
          SMU 38 BYU 25

Johnson kicks off to L.McIlhenny at 42 (Shell)

     SMU 4:07
     1-10 C-42 James around left end for 42 yard TD
1 plays 42 yards Elapsed Time 11:03 Garcia PAT good   SMU 45 BYU 25

Garcia kicks off to Hansen at 18 retrun to 28 for 10 (Nichols, Godine)

BYU 3:58

1-10 C-28 McMahon runs for 14 to 42 (Ferguson)   FIRST DOWN RUSHI
1-10 C-42 McMahon pass intended for L.Jones, incomplete (Prested, R.Carter)
2-10 C-42 McMahon pass complete to Lane for 8 to 50 (McAfee)
3- 2 50   McMahon pass complete to Phillips for 10 to 40 (Douglas) FIRST DOWN PASS
1-10 M-40 McMahon pass intended for Phillips, incomplete (B.Smith)
2-10 M-40 McMahon pass complete to C.Brown for 25 to 15 (R.Carter) FIRST DOWN PASS
1-10 M-15 McMahon pass complete to Braga for 15 yard TD

7 plays 72 yards McMahon pass incomplete to Phillips PAT no good Elapsed Time 12:27
     SMU 45 BYU 31

Johnson kicks off to (on sides kick recovered by Shell at 50

BYU 2:31
1-10 50   McMahon pass complete to Pettis for 9 to 41 (R.Carter)
2- 1 M-41 McMahon pass intended for Braga, incomplete (pass tipped by Bennett)
3- 1 M-41 McMahon pass complete to B.Davis for 40 to 1 (Hopkins)   FIRST DOWN PASS
1- G M- 1 Phillips around right end for 1 yard TD
4 plays 50 yards   Elapsed Time 13:02 McMahon pass complete to Phillips for 2 point PAT
          SMU 45 BYU 39
Johnson kicks off to Blaylock at C-47 (Shell)

     SMU 1:57
     1-10 C-47 Dickerson up middle for loss of 1 to 48 (Whittingham)
     2- 9 C-48 McIlhenny around right end for 3 to 45 (Redd)
     3- 6 C-45 1:06 Dickerson at left end for 2 to 43 (Schoepflin)
     4- 4 C-43 0:18 delay of game SMU
     4- 9 C-48 0:18 Kaifes punt blocked by Schoepflin
                Kaifes recovers at M-41
BYU 0:13
1-10 M-41 0:13 McMahon pass intended for C.Brown, incomplete
2-10 M-41 McMahon pass intended for L.Jones, incomplete (Blaylock)
3-10 M-41 0:03 McMahon pass complete in end zone for C.Brown for 41 yard TD

3 plays 41 yards Elapsed Time 15:00 Gunther PAT good BYU 46 SMU 45
          END OF GAME 9:41 PM PST   BYU COUGARS 46   SMU MUSTANGS 45

3RD DOWN CONV

BYU   SMU
3/4   0/2

National Collegiate Athletic Association
QUICKIE STATISTICS

First Quarter   Half   Third Quarter   (Final)

(Circle One)

TEAM

	SOUTHERN METHODIST Visitors	BRIGHAM YOUNG Home Team
Score	45	46
First Downs	25	23
Rushes—Yardage (Net)	66 - 393	24 (-2)
Passing Yardage (Net)	53	446
*Return Yardage (Net)	0	98
Passes—Att.-Comp.-Int.	11 - 6 - 0	49 - 32 - 1
Total Offense—Yards	446	444
Punts (Number-Average)	4 - 155 - 38.8	5 - 163 - 32.6
Fumbles—Lost	2 - 0	2 - 0
Penalties—Yards	7 - 65	8 - 80

*Return of Punts, Intercepted Passes and Fumbles (not kickoffs).

INDIVIDUAL LEADERS

SOUTHERN METHODIST — Visitors

Rushing	Att.	Net Yards	TD	Long
JAMES	23	225	2	45
DICKERSON	23	110	2	28

Passing	Att.-Comp.-Int.	Yds.	TD
McILHENNY	11-6-0	53	1

Pass Receiving	No.	Yards	TD	Long
JAMES	2	13	1	10
A. SMITH	1	10	0	10
M. BENNETT	1	20	0	20

Punting	No.	Avg.	Long
KALFES	4	38.8	51

BRIGHAM YOUNG — Home Team

Rushing	Att.	Net Yards	TD	Long
S. PHILLIPS	8	18	2	9
McMAHON	10	0	0	20
LANE	4	-2	0	1

Passing	Att.-Comp.-Int.	Yds.	TD
McMAHON	49-32-1	446	4

Pass Receiving	No.	Yards	TD	Long
S. PHILLIPS	10	81	0	14
C. BROWN	5	155	3	64
BRAGA	5	77	1	22

Punting	No.	Avg.	Long
C. BROWN	5	32.6	35

151

National Collegiate Athletic Association
DEFENSIVE STATISTICS

Player BRIGHAM YOUNG (Team)	Tackles			for Loss	Fumb Rcvd	Pass Inte	Pass Brkp
	UT	AT	Tot				
5 PRESTED	4	4	8				
12 BRADY	3		3				
22 JELISELI	1		1				
38 ED ST. PIERRE	1	9	10				
41 REDD	9	5	14	1			
43 SCHOEPFLIN	4	4	8				2
46 HOLMOE	5	3	8				
59 WHITTINGHAM	10	6	16				
76 TITENSOR	3	7	10				
78 EHIN	4		4	1			
86 PLATER	1		1				
93 ANAE, B	5	3	8				
14 WALKER	1		1				
17 WILSON	1		1				
32 JAMES					1		
77 MORGAN	2	2	4				
79 SMITH	1		1				
54 SHELL	2		2				

UNOFFICIAL SACKS - TEAM

REDD - 1 - 9YDS

EHIN - 1 - 6YDS

2 TOTAL

43 SCHOEPFLIN - BLOCKED PUNT

National Collegiate Athletic Association
DEFENSIVE STATISTICS

Player	SOUTHERN METHODIST (Team)	Tackles			for Loss	Fumb Rcvd	Pass Into	
		UT	AT	Tot				
55	MOTELL	4	3	7	2			
74	CARTER, M	5	2	7	2			
75	ARMSTRONG	5	4	9	3			
27	BRUTON	7		7			1	
34	SIMMONS					1		
36	BENNETT	5	1	6				
93	WASHINGTON	1		1				
80	HOLT, B	3	1	4				
66	THEUS	1		1				
20	HORLEY	2	2	4				
5	PHILLIPS	2		2				
97	SIMON	1		1				
23	SMITH, B	1		1	1			
29	CARTER, P			2				
58	CHANEY	1						
25	BLAYLOCK	1	1	2				
18	LILLY	1		1	1			
30	GODWE		1	1				
8	NICHOLS		1	1				
99	FERGUSON	1						
64	MEAFEE	1		1				
91	DOUGLAS	1		1				
46	HOPKINS	1		1				

UNOFFICIAL SACKS - TEAM
CARTER   2 - 4.4 YDS
ARMSTRONG 2 - 16.10 YDS
SMITH, B   1 - 9 YDS
LILLY   1 - 7 YDS
TOTAL

NOTES

INTRODUCTION

1. Dave Hatz, "'Hail Mary' Pass Results in 'Mormon Miracle' as BYU Slips Past Mustangs," *Daily Californian*, December 20, 1980.

2. "BYU Prayer Answered with 'Hail Mary' Pass," *Wisconsin State Journal*, December 21, 1980.

3. "'Hail Mary' Pass Clinches BYU's First Bowl Victory," *Atlanta Journal*, December 21, 1980.

4. Bill Finley, "Saints Get a 'Miracle' to Win 46-45," *San Diego Union*, December 20, 1980.

5. "BYU Victory Hailed as Holiday Miracle," *Arizona Republic*, December 21, 1980.

6. Lee Benson, Sports Column, "Houdini Bowl," *Deseret News*.

7. "Do You Believe in Miracles? BYU Does," *San Diego Tribune*, December 20, 1980.

8. Dave Hatz, "'Hail Mary' Pass Results in 'Mormon Miracle' as BYU Slips Past Mustangs," *Daily Californian*, December 20, 1980.

9. "The 10 Best Plays," *Sports Illustrated Football's Greatest* (Sports Illustrated, 2012), 194.

CHAPTER 2

1. "How It All Began," *1980 Holiday Bowl Kickoff Luncheon Program*.

2. Ibid.

3. Bruce Binkowski, in conversation with author in the Holdiay Bowl offices, September 2013.

4. SMUMustangs.com, "90 Greatest Moments in SMU Football History," accessed October 16, 2014, http://www.smumustangs.com/sports/m-footbl/spec-rel/greatest-moments-78.html.

5. Ibid.

6. Tom Holmoe, email message to author.

7. Jim McMahon, email message to author.

8. ESPN Films, *30 for 30: Pony Excess*, back cover, directed by Thaddeus D. Matula, (Team Marketing, 2011), DVD.

9. ESPN Films, *30 for 30: Pony Excess*, directed by Thaddeus D. Matula, (Team Marketing, 2011), DVD.

10. Ibid.

11. Ibid.

12. Steve Bisheff, *San Diego Union*, November 13, 1980.

13. John Mooney, "Utes Entertain Cougars, Hopes for Holiday Bowl," *Salt Lake Tribune*, November 22, 1980.

14. John Mooney, "Cougars Plaster Utes, 56-6, as McMahon Leads March to WAC Title and Holiday Bowl Game," *Salt Lake Tribune*, November 23, 1980.

15. John Mooney, *Salt Lake Tribune*, November 17, 1980.

CHAPTER 3

1. Steve Bisheff, "The Fantasy Bowl," *San Diego Union*, December 20, 1980.

2. Mike Monroe, "Cougars Must Whip Bowl Hex or Face Credibility Doubts," *Denver Post*, November 29, 1980.

3. "Can Cougars Shake Bowl Jinx?" *Provo Daily Herald*.

4. Lee Benson, Sports Column, "Holiday on Hold," *Deseret News*.

5. Ray Scott, *1980 Holiday Bowl Game Broadcast*, December 19, 1980.

CHAPTER 4

1. LaVell Edwards, in conversation with author.

Chapter 5

1. Marion Dunn, "Holland, Edwards Tickle Ears at Kick-Off Luncheon," *Provo Daily Herald*, December 18, 1980.

Chapter 6

1. Ish Haley, "When SMU needs the Big Play," *Third Annual San Diego Holiday Bowl Program*, December 19, 1980.

2. "Clay Brown—The Complete Tight End," *Third Annual San Diego Holiday Bowl Program*, December 19, 1980.

3. Ron Meyer, in Ish Haley "When SMU needs the Big Play," *Third Annual San Diego Holiday Bowl Program*, December 19, 1980.

4. Ray Scott, *1980 Holiday Bowl Game Broadcast*, December 19, 1980.

5. Grady Alderman, *1980 Holiday Bowl Game Broadcast*, December 19, 1980.

6. Craig James, quoted by Ed Zieralski, *Daily Californian*, December 20, 1980.

7. Ray Scott, *1980 Holiday Bowl Game Broadcast*, December 19, 1980.

8. Grady Alderman, *1980 Holiday Bowl Game Broadcast*, December 19, 1980.

9. Ray Scott, *1980 Holiday Bowl Game Broadcast*, December 19, 1980.

10. Nick Canepa, "'Phantom Catch' Ignites Cougars' Comeback," *San Diego Tribune*, December 20, 1980.

11. "Last Gasp TD Gives Cougars First Bowl Win," *Provo Daily Herald*.

12. Marion Dunn, "Don Shaw Almost Called the Shot Perfectly," *Provo Daily Herald*.

13. Scott Phillips, in conversation with author.

14. Matt Braga, email message to author.

15. Lee Johnson, in conversation with author.

16. Scott Phillips, in conversation with author.

17. Ibid.

18. Tony Roberts, *Radio Broadcast for 1980 Miracle Bowl*, December 19, 1980.

19. Ron Meyer, quoted in Wayne Lockwood "Incredible! Sure, It's the Holiday Bowl," *San Diego Union*, December 20, 1980.

20. Clay Brown, in conversation with author.

21. Clay Brown, *Holiday Bowl 25th Anniversary Game Program*.

22. Ray Scott, *1980 Holiday Bowl Game Broadcast*, December 19, 1980.

23. Kurt Gunther, in conversation with author.

24. Bob Hudson, *Provo Daily Herald*.

25. Ray Herbat, "Call 'Em Nuts or Special," *Salt Lake Tribune*, December 16, 1980.

26. Ibid.

27. Bill Schoepflin, in conversation with author.

28. Kurt Gunther, in conversation with author.

29. Ray Scott, *1980 Holiday Bowl Game Broadcast*, December 19, 1980.

CHAPTER 8

1. Ray Scott, *1980 Holiday Bowl Game Broadcast*, December 19, 1980.

2. Tony Roberts, *Radio Broadcast for 1980 Miracle Bowl*, December 19, 1980.

3. Ibid.

4. "Best Bowls of All Time," *TV Guide*, December 28, 1996.

5. ESPN.com, "College Football's Fantastic Finishes," SportsNation, last updated November 20, 2002, accessed November 21, 2002, http://sports.espn.go.com/espn/print?id=1463173&type=Story.

6. ESPN.com, "The List: Greatest Bowl Games," accessed December 28, 2011, http://espn.go.com/page2/s/list/bestbowls.html.

7. Youtube.com, "Greatest Bowl Comeback Ever? 1980 Holiday Bowl: BYU vs. SMU," accessed October 17, 2014, https://www.youtube.com/watch?v=b55Tn_YbLK8.

8. Pete Fiutak, "Where Does the 2007 Fiesta Bowl Rank?" CollegeFootballNews.com, accessed October 17, 2014, http://cfn.scout.com/2/606020.html.

9. Tina Sans, "10 Most Dramatic Bowl Games of All Time—NCAA College Football," last updated January 3, 2011, accessed October 17, 2014, http://www.deepintosports.com/2011/01/03/10-most-dramatic-bowl-games-of-all-time-ncaa-college-football/

10. A. J. Floss, "Do you Believe in Miracles? Top 20 'Miracles' in Sports History," SportsThenandNow.com, last updated February 22, 2011, accessed October 17, 2014, http://sportsthenandnow.com/2011/02/22/do-you-believe-in-miracles-top-20-miracles-in-sports-history/.

11. Dan Vasta, "50 Most Exciting College Football Bowl Games of All Time," accessed October 17, 2014, http://bleacherreport.com/articles/983921-50-best-college-football-bowl-programs-in-history.

12. "BYU Football: Top 50 Plays," BYUtv, August 2013.

13. Matt Brown, "Best College Football Hail Marys," sportsonearth.com, last updated September 22, 2014, accessed October 17, 2014, http://www.sportsonearth.com/article/95864112/ranking-college-footballs-greatest-hail-mary-finishes.

14. Bruce Binkowski, in coversation with author.

Chapter 10

1. Youtube.com, "Greatest Bowl Comeback Ever? 1980 Holiday Bowl: BYU vs. SMU," accessed October 17, 2014, https://www.youtube.com/watch?v=b55Tn_YbLK8.

Where Are They Now?

1. Vai Sikahema, in coversation with author.

2. Ibid.

3. Glen Titensor, in conversation with author.

4. Bart Oates, in conversation with author.

5. Matt Braga, in conversation with author.

6. Eric Lane, in conversation with author.

7. Lloyd Eldredge, in conversation with author.

8. Kurt Gunther, in conversation with author.

9. Mark Gowans and Clay Brown, in conversation with author.

10. Ron Meyer, in "2004 Hall of Fame Inductee—1984 National Championship Football Team," accessed October 17, 2014, http://byucougars.com/athlete/m-football/1984-national-championship-football-team.

RYAN E. TIBBITTS

Ryan Tibbitts is a graduate of Ricks College, Brigham Young University, and the J. Reuben Clark Law School. While at BYU, he was a member of two WAC championship football teams, including the 1980 Miracle Bowl team. Ryan has practiced law in Utah for thirty years and is currently in-house counsel for Qualtrics International. He also consults with other businesses on litigation and dispute resolution issues. He resides near Park City, Utah, with his wife and five children.